Cloud 9-1 GCSE REVISION NOTES FOR WILLIAM SHAKESPEARE'S *THE MERCHANT OF VENICE*

Study guide (with AQA-style sample assessment questions and notes)

by Joe Broadfoot MA

ISBN-13: 978-1548451899

ISBN-10: 1548451894

DEDICATION

To all GCSE students, who want to be on 'cloud nine' come results day!
Cloud 9-1 is here to help you move from grade 1 or above to 9.

CONTENTS

ACKNOWLEDGMENTS

A big thank you to those who have supported in me in my career and also thanks to those that haven't, as your negativity changes to something more positive.

1 AQA-STYLE EXAM QUESTIONS & NOTES

AQA-STYLE EXAM QUESTIONS & NOTES

#1

AQA-style Specimen Assessment Material 1: The Merchant of Venice

Read the following extract from Act 2 Scene 8 of The Merchant of Venice and then answer the question that follows.

Starting with this conversation, explore how Shakespeare presents attitudes towards Shylock in The Merchant of Venice.
Write about:
• how Shakespeare demonstrates Salanio and Salarino's attitudes towards Shylock in this conversation
• how Shakespeare presents attitudes towards Shylock in the play as a whole.

At this point in the play, Salanio and Salarino are discussing Shylock's reaction to Jessica's elopement. This extract is important because it gives the audience an idea of what the general public think of Shylock.

EXTRACT

SALANIO
I never heard a passion so confused,
So strange, outrageous, and so variable,
As the dog Jew did utter in the streets:
'My daughter! O my ducats! O my daughter!
Fled with a Christian! O my Christian ducats!
Justice! the law! my ducats, and my daughter!
A sealed bag, two sealed bags of ducats,

Comment [JB(]: AO2 – The writer's use of a tetracolon emphasises passionate Shylock's was in Salanio's opinion. The cumulation of adjectives make Shylock appear impossible to understand, so consumed is he with emotion. The hyperbole of 'never' adds to the idea that

Comment [JB(]: AO2 – Dog imagery is used to describe Shylock, not for the first or last time in the play. This shows that Venetians see Shylock as down-at-heel like a dog, possibly with the tendency to become a vicious brute.
AO3 – Although sixteenth-century Venice

Comment [JB(]: AO1 – Although Salanio seems to attempt to directly quote from Shylock's speech, we can sense that it has been exaggerated to mock the Jew.
AO2 – The use of alliteration emphasises how upset Shylock is at the discovery that he daughter has run off with his money.

Comment [JB(]: AO2 – the repetition of 'O' makes a mockery out of Shylock's grief. Structurally, the exclamation marks add to the sense that this account is exaggerated and probably inaccurate.
AO3 – Being a Jew, it is highly unlikely that Shylock would refer to the ducats as

Comment [JB(]: AO1 – Shylock may be appealing for justice, but it is difficult to imagine he will receive it in this prejudiced society.

Comment [JB(]: AO2 – The repetition of the possessive pronoun 'my' adds to the idea that Shylock is concerned about what he owns. Now that he has lost his daughter and a considerable amount of money, he may well be in a state of mourning.

Comment [JB(]: AO2 – The bawdy imagery is repeated later, as in this parody of Shylock's speech (which we, as an audience, are not party to), the Jew feels as if he has been kicked in his genital area.

1

Of double ducats, stolen from me by my daughter!
And jewels, two stones, two rich and precious stones,
Stolen by my daughter! Justice! find the girl;
She hath the stones upon her, and the ducats.'

SALARINO
Why, all the boys in Venice follow him,
Crying, his stones, his daughter, and his ducats.

SALANIO
Let good Antonio look he keep his day,
Or he shall pay for this.

#2

AQA-style Specimen Assessment Material 2: The Merchant of Venice
Read the following extract from Act 1 Scene 3 of *The Merchant of Venice* and then answer the question that follows.

Starting with this speech, how does Shakespeare present Shylock's feelings about the way he is treated? Write about:
• how Shakespeare presents Shylock in this speech
• how Shakespeare presents Shylock in the play as a whole.

At this point in the play, Shylock is speaking to Antonio. Antonio has asked Shylock to lend him some money. This extract is important because it is the first time we hear of the prejudice that is endured by Shylock.

EXTRACT

SHYLOCK
Signior Antonio, many a time and oft
In the Rialto you have rated me
About my monies and my usances.
Still have I borne it with a patient shrug
For suff'rance is the badge of all our tribe.
You call me misbeliever, cut-throat dog,
And spit upon my Jewish gaberdine,
And all for use of that which is mine own.
Well then, it now appears you need my help.
Go to, then, you come to me, and you say,
'Shylock, we would have monies' – you say so,

Comment [JB(]: AO1 – Salarino's mocking tone is similar to Salanio, hence the almost identical names. They represent the typical businessmen of sixteenth-century Venice in that have no

Comment [JB(]: AO1 – The extract ends with Salanio warning that Antonio might have to 'pay' for Shylock's grief. Later on in the play, we discover that Salanio is right about that, as Shylock demands his

Comment [JB(]: AO2 – Shylock begins his speech in a respectful manner, by calling Antonio 'signior', which equates to mister. This makes Shylock seem like a humble person.

Comment [JB(]: AO2 – The alliterative 'r' sound creates an effect of a growling dog. This makes Shylock appear to switch from a respectful person into something more animalistic, when angered by his

Comment [JB(]: AO3 – Usury, or lending money at extortionate rates of interest, was a banned activity for Christians. Jews provided that service for those that wanted it, but were largely condemned

Comment [JB(]: AO1 – Shylock tells us that he has been patient in the face of persecution and prejudice, simply shrugging it off.

Comment [JB(]: AO2 – This metaphor emphasises how awful the discrimination is. He equates being a Jew with 'suff'rance'.
AO3 – Actually, Jew were required to

Comment [JB(]: AO2 – Dog imagery creates the idea that Shylock is treated like an animal because of his religion, which is referred to by the word 'misbeliever'. The adjective 'cut-throat'

Comment [JB(]: AO1 – Shylock, anecdotally, accuses Antonio of spitting on his Jewish robe. The lack of a reply from Antonio, implies that: either it is true, or that he does not want to

Comment [JB(]: AO2 – Shylock repeats the word 'And' which simply but effectively lists all the insults and degradation that he has had to endure.

You that did void your rheum upon my beard,
And foot me as you spurn a stranger cur
Over your threshold: monies is your suit.
What should I say to you? Should I not say
'Hath a dog money? Is it possible
A cur can lend three thousand ducats?' Or
Shall I bend low, and in a bondman's key,
With bated breath and whisp'ring humbleness,
Say this: 'Fair sir, you spit on me on Wednesday last,
You spurned me such a day, another time
You called me dog: and for these courtesies
I'll lend you thus much monies.'

#3

AQA-style Specimen Assessment Material 3: The Merchant of Venice
Read the following extract from Act 3 Scene 4 of *The Merchant of Venice* and then answer the question that follows.

Starting with this speech, explore how far Shakespeare presents Portia as a strong female character in The Merchant of Venice.
Write about:
• how Shakespeare presents Portia in this speech
• how far Shakespeare presents Portia as a strong female character in the play as a whole.

At this point in the play, Portia is talking about the disguise she is going to wear. This extract is important because it is the first time that we see Portia as active rather than passive. She is literally going to take the law into her own hands in a male-dominated world and needs a disguise in order to do so.

EXTRACT

PORTIA
They shall, Nerissa; but in such a habit,
That they shall think we are accomplished
With that we lack. I'll hold thee any wager,
When we are both accoutred like young men,
I'll prove the prettier fellow of the two,
And wear my dagger with the braver grace,
And speak between the change of man and boy
With a reed voice, and turn two mincing steps
Into a manly stride, and speak of frays

Comment [JB(]: AO1 – Shylock rephrases his anecdote about being spat on. This time, he claims that Antonio spat on his beard. This means that either this

Comment [JB(]: AO2 – Dog imagery of the word 'cur' makes Shylock appear to be down-at-heel, at the level of an animal. Shylock uses the noun 'foot' as a

Comment [JB(]: AO2 – Shylock uses rhetorical questions to persuasively put forward his point of view that he has been mistreated.

Comment [JB(]: AO1 – Shylock's anger aand resentment is apparent here as he believes he has been treated no better than a slave or bondsman.

Comment [JB(]: AO2 – The alliterative phrase 'bated breath' usually suggests excitement, like a dog might feel waiting for its master. However, this phrase is

Comment [JB(]: AO1 – Shylock mocks himself in this speech, as he imagines being more humble and less resentful than he is.

Comment [JB(]: AO2 – The word 'habit' relates to the theme of religion, although Portia means they will wear a male disguise to circumvent gender prejudice.

Comment [JB(]: AO1 – This is a bawdy reference to their lack of male genitalia and makes it apparent that they feel that superficial difference has stopped them

Comment [JB(]: AO1 – Portia is bragging and making it seem like she is already turning into a man, by taking on their negative qualities.

Comment [JB(]: AO1 – Portia mocks men, by suggesting that they are unnecessarily competitive. She clearly thinks even their fashion sense is

Comment [JB(]: AO2 – The word 'and' is repeated, listing the numerous boasts of a typical male.

Like a fine bragging youth, and tell quaint lies,
How honourable ladies sought my love,
Which I denying, they fell sick and died;
I could not do withal; then I'll repent,
And wish for all that, that I had not killed them;
And twenty of these puny lies I'll tell,
That men shall swear I have discontinued school
Above a twelvemonth. I have within my mind
A thousand raw tricks of these bragging Jacks,
Which I will practise.

> **Comment [JB(]:** AO2 – The simile is ironic, as Portia calls this imaginary youth 'fine', but really he is nothing but a lying braggart.

> **Comment [JB(]:** AO2 – Portia uses hyperbole for comic effect here, as she is still mocking how men have a habit of making ridiculous unsubstantiated claims.

> **Comment [JB(]:** AO1 – Portia clearly believes that the male-dominated world thrives on lies.

> **Comment [JB(]:** AO2 – Portia exaggerates when she says she has 'a thousand raw tricks', aping how men behave when they are bragging.

> **Comment [JB(]:** AO1 – The verb 'over-name' meant 'list' and implies that Portia is unimpressed with the number of suitors that are hoping to win the casket test.
> AO2 – She is speaking in prose, which is unusual for aristocratic Shakespearean characters, as they normally speak in verse. This suggests that the content of her speeches will be more in keeping with the bawdy conversations of lower classes.

#4

AQA-style Specimen Assessment Material 4: The Merchant of Venice
Read the following extract from Act 1 Scene 2 of *The Merchant of Venice* and then answer the question that follows.

Starting with this speech, explore how Shakespeare presents Portia's feelings towards her suitors.
Write about:
• how Shakespeare presents Portia's feelings towards her suitors in this speech
• how Shakespeare presents Portia's feelings towards her suitors in the play as a whole.

At this point in the play, Portia is complaining because she cannot choose her own husband. Unfortunately for her, her father's will prevents her from doing so.
Instead, there are a number of suitors, who are hoping to win her hand in marriage and her dowry, by choosing the right casket.
This extract is important because we see Portia's witty reaction to some unwanted suitors.

EXTRACT

PORTIA
I pray thee over-name them, and as thou namest them I will describe them – and according to my description level at my affection.

NERISSA
First, there is the Neapolitan prince.

PORTIA

Ay, that's a colt indeed, for he doth nothing but talk of his horse – and he makes it a great appropriation to his own good parts, that he can shoe him himself. I am much afeard my lady his mother played false with a smith.

NERISSA
Then is there the County Palatine.

PORTIA
He doth nothing but frown – as who should say 'An you will not have me, choose.' He hears merry tales and smiles not. I fear he will prove the weeping philosopher when he grows old, being so full of unmannerly sadness in his youth. I had rather be married to a death's-head with a bone in his mouth than to either of these. God defend me from these two!

NERISSA
How say you by the French lord, Monsieur Le Bon?

PORTIA
God made him, and therefore let him pass for a man. In truth I know it is a sin to be a mocker, but he! – Why he hath a horse better than the Neapolitan's, a better bad habit of frowning than the Count Palatine: he is every man in no man. If a throstle sing, he falls straight a-capering. He will fence with his own shadow. If I should marry him, I should marry twenty husbands. If he would despise me I would forgive him – for if he love me to madness, I shall never requite him.

#5

AQA-style Specimen Assessment Material 5: The Merchant of Venice
Read the following extract from Act 1 Scene 3 of *The Merchant of Venice* and then answer the question that follows.

Starting with this speech, explore how Shakespeare presents the relationship between Shylock and Antonio. Write about:
• how Shakespeare presents the relationship between Shylock and Antonio.
• how Shakespeare presents the relationship between Shylock and Antonio in the play as a whole.

Comment [JB(]: AO1 – Portia complains that he is obsessed with his horse. This

Comment [JB(]: AO1 – Portia believes that the Neapolitan prince is a braggart,

Comment [JB(]: AO2 – Portia uses 'much afeard' ironically, as the reverse is

Comment [JB(]: AO1 – Portia casts aspersions over the Neapolitan prince's

Comment [JB(]: AO1 – Portia's view of the County Palatine is he is too miserable

Comment [JB(]: AO1 – This implies that Portia wants the man in her life to have a

Comment [JB(]: AO1 – Portia predicts that the County Palatine will be crying

Comment [JB(]: AO1 – Portia makes her distaste for both certain plain. Marriage

Comment [JB(]: AO3 – In 1596 (which was around the date when the play was

Comment [JB(]: AO1 – Portia is just as dismissive of Monsieur Le Bon, the French

Comment [JB(]: AO1 – Portia may feel a tiny bit guilty that she has nothing good

Comment [JB(]: AO1 – The French prince, in her opinion, is likely to be more

Comment [JB(]: AO2 – Portia uses hyperbole for comic effect, suggesting

Comment [JB(]: AO2 – Although it is a songbird, the word 'throstle' does not

Comment [JB(]: AO1 – Portia describes the French lord's dancing as 'a-capering',

Comment [JB(]: AO1 – Portia makes it clear that the French lord is forever

Comment [JB(]: AO2 – Portia's mocking tone is evident in her use of hyperbole.

Comment [JB(]: AO1 – Portia's extreme reaction to the French lord is evident, as

At this point in the play, Antonio is coming to Shylock to borrow money. This extract is important because we see Shylock's reaction to a Christian, who has wronged him in the past.

EXTRACT

BASSANIO
This is Signor Antonio.

SHYLOCK *(aside)*
How like a fawning publican he looks!
I hate him for he is a Christian –
But more, for that in low simplicity
He lends out money gratis, and brings down
The rate of usance here with us in Venice.
If I can catch him once upon the hip,
I will feed fat the ancient grudge I bear him.
He hates our sacred nation, and he rails,
Even there where merchants most do congregate,
On me, my bargains, and my well-won thrift,
Which he calls interest. Cursed be my tribe
If I forgive him!

BASSANIO
Shylock, do you hear?

SHYLOCK
I am debating of my present store,
And by the near guess of my memory
I cannot instantly raise up the gross
Of full three thousand ducats. What of that?
Tubal, a wealthy Hebrew of my tribe,
Will furnish me. But soft! – how many months
Do you desire? *(To Antonio)* Rest you fair, good signor –
Your worship was the last man in our mouths.

ANTONIO
Shylock, albeit I neither lend nor borrow
By taking nor by giving of excess,
Yet to supply the ripe wants of my friend,
I'll break a custom. *(To Bassanio)* Is he yet possessed
How much ye would?

#6

Comment [JB(]: AO2 – Shakespeare uses this dramatic device to allow the audience to see inside Shylock's mind. This makes him a more sympathetic

Comment [JB(]: AO2 – The use of the simile comparing Antonio to the taxman implies that to Shylock his arrival is just as unwelcome. It may also suggest that the

Comment [JB(]: AO1 – Shylock is straightforward and to the point as he clearly states how much he despises Antonio.

Comment [JB(]: AO1 – Shylock's business is affected by Antonio's tendency to lend money without charging interest. Clearly, Shylock feels Antonio

Comment [JB(]: AO1 – Shylock is clearly planning his revenge, as he uses this phrase to imply that he wants to catch Antonio off balance.

Comment [JB(]: AO2 – The alliteration of 'feed fat' is disconcerting as the repeating 'f' sound makes it appear that Shylock is swearing. This is combined with

Comment [JB(]: AO1 – Shylock is retaliating, as he is unlikely to have an 'ancient grudge' against someone has not wronged

Comment [JB(]: AO3 – Hatred for Jews was commonplace, at the time. Not long before the play was first performed (in 1594), a Portuguese physician-in-chief

Comment [JB(]: AO2 – The word 'tribe' makes Shylock's identification with Judaism sound tribal and therefore primitive. It makes the audience

Comment [JB(]: AO1 – This line shows how devious Shylock is, as he does not want Bassanio and Antonio to know what he has really been thinking about. He

Comment [JB(]: AO2 – Shylock's tone is much more polite and business-like in conversation and he is using words that relate to finance such as 'gross'. The

Comment [JB(]: AO2 – Shylock's hyperbolic greeting to Antonio shows him to be a two-faced liar, as the 'worship' of Antonio was not something he has talked

Comment [JB(]: AO1 – Antonio clearly states his intention to borrow, even if it means paying interest, for the sake of Bassanio. The juxtaposition against the

AQA-style Specimen Assessment Material 6: The Merchant of Venice
Read the following extract from Act 1 Scene 1 of *The Merchant of Venice* and then answer the question that follows.

Starting with this speech, explore how Shakespeare presents the relationship between Bassanio and Antonio.
Write about:
• how Shakespeare presents the relationship between Bassanio and Antonio in the extract.
• how Shakespeare presents the relationship between Bassanio and Antonio in the play as a whole.

At this point in the play, Bassanio is visiting Antonio to ask for a loan. This extract is important because we see how close the relationship is between Antonio and Bassanio, which is vital as it drives the plot forwards.

EXTRACT

ANTONIO
Well, tell me now what lady is the same
To whom you swore a secret pilgrimage,
That you today promised to tell me of.

BASSANIO
'Tis not unknown to you, Antonio,
How much I have disabled mine estate
By something showing a more swelling port
Than my faint means would grant continuance.
Nor do I now make moan to be abridged
From such a noble rate – but my chief care
Is to come fairly off from the great debts
Wherein my time something too prodigal
Hath left me gaged. To you, Antonio,
I owe the most, in money and in love,
And from your love I have a warranty
To unburden all my plots and purposes
How to get clear of all the debts I owe.

ANTONIO
I pray you, good Bassanio, let me know it –
And if it stand, as you yourself still do,
Within the eye of honour, be assured

Comment [JB(]: AO2 – Structurally, Shakespeare has waited until now to reveal what may be the source of Antonio's sadness at the very beginning.

Comment [JB(]: AO1 – Quite why this love is 'secret' from Antonio gives the audience something to ponder. Is Bassanio worried about hurting Antonio's

Comment [JB(]: AO1: Bassanio's response seems quite hesitant, as it takes him a long time to name Portia. Perhaps he is worried about Antonio's response.

Comment [JB(]: AO1 – Bassanio begins by telling Antonio what he already knows: that he has squandered what wealth he had.

Comment [JB(]: AO2 – Bassanio's speech contains a nautical metaphor that links his fortune to that of a sea 'port'. This foreshadows how Antonio's business

Comment [JB(]: AO1 – Bassanio's lack of financial clout means he has to rely on Antonio for money. It shows their respective statuses are unequal, like a

Comment [JB(]: AO2 – The use of alliteration here adds to the sense that Bassanio's finances are enough to make someone cry out.

Comment [JB(]: AO1 – Bassanio, albeit long-windedly, is spelling out his intention to free himself from debt.

Comment [JB(]: AO2 – Using direct address, Bassanio appeals directly to Antonio, praising him for the love and money he has given him in the past.

Comment [JB(]: AO1 – Bassanio appears to be treading very carefully, explaining that because of Antonio's love, he feels compelled to tell him the whole truth

Comment [JB(]: AO1 – Antonio is eager to help his friend. He is almost begging Bassanio to reveal all, by using the religious verb 'pray' although, at the time,

Comment [JB(]: AO2 – The only proviso made by Antonio is that Bassanio's proposed enterprise should be metaphorically 'within eye of honour'.

My purse, my person, my extremest means
Lie all unlocked to your occasions.

BASSANIO
In my school-days, when I had lost one shaft,
I shot his fellow of the self-same flight
The self-same way, with more advised watch
To find the other forth, and by adventuring both
I oft found both. I urge this childhood proof
Because what follows is pure innocence.
I owe you much, and, like a wilful youth
That which I owe is lost. But if you please
To shoot another arrow that self way
Which you did shoot the first, I do not doubt,
As I will watch the aim, or to find both
Or bring your latter hazard back again,
And thankfully rest debtor for the first.

Comment [JB(]: AO2 – Antonio's use of an ascending tricolon shows us the lengths he will go to accommodate his friend. His 'purse' sounds smaller than his 'person', which is turn gazumped by his

Comment [JB(]: AO1 – Bassanio talks about when he was younger and the lessons he learned then. It makes him appear to be older and wiser than he once was.

Comment [JB(]: AO2 – The use of repetition and sibilance in Bassanio's speech ('self-same') gives the impression that by making slight variations one can learn from mistakes.

Comment [JB(]: AO1 – Bassanio is being quite convincing, trying to urge Antonio to loan him more money, so that all the money owed can be returned.
AO2 – Bassanio cleverly uses the analogy

Comment [JB(]: AO1 – Bassanio is desperately trying to cast himself in a positive light, in order to obtain the loan.

Comment [JB(]: AO1 – This shows the balance of power in their relationship. Clearly, Antonio is Bassanio's father figure and generous benefactor.

Comment [JB(]: AO2 – The simile of the 'wilful youth' emphasises how Bassanio realises how he has been at fault in the past, losing evey penny that has been loaned to him previously. The word

Comment [JB(]: AO2 – The use of repetition of the 'arrow' imagery reinforces Bassanio's argument that to lend him more money would result in all Antonio's 'lost' riches being restored to

Comment [JB(]: AO1 – Bassanio believes that the worst-case scenario is he will be able to pay back the money he is about to borrow, even if he cannot recover the money that he has already

#7

AQA-style Specimen Assessment Material 7: The Merchant of Venice
Read the following extract from Act 5 Scene 1 of *The Merchant of Venice* and then answer the question that follows.

Starting with this speech, explore how Shakespeare presents married couples.
Write about:
• how Shakespeare presents the relationship between married couples in the extract.
• how Shakespeare presents the relationship between married couples in the play as a whole.

At this point in the play, Portia and Nerissa have just arrived back in a moonlit Belmont to greet their returning husbands (Bassanio and Gratiano, respectively) and Antonio (visiting for the first time). Nerissa has 'discovered' that Gratiano is no longer wearing her ring and seeks an explanation. This extract is important because Shakespeare uses dramatic irony here to create humour.

EXTRACT

GRATIANO [*To Nerissa*] By yonder moon I swear you do
me wrong;
In faith, I gave it to the judge's clerk;
Would he were gelt that had it, for my part,
Since you do take it, love, so much at heart.

PORTIA: A quarrel, ho, already! what's the matter?

GRATIANO: About a hoop of gold, a paltry ring
That she did give me, whose posy was
For all the world like cutler's poetry
Upon a knife, 'Love me, and leave me not'.

NERISSA: What talk you of the posy, or the value?
You swore to me, when I did give it you,
That you would wear it till your hour of death,
And that it should lie with you in your grave:
Though not for me, yet for your vehement oaths,
You should have been respective and have kept it.
Gave it a judge's clerk! no, God's my judge,
The clerk will ne'er wear hair on's face that had it.

GRATIANO: He will, and if he live to be a man.

NERISSA: Ay, if a woman live to be a man.

GRATIANO: Now, by this hand, I gave it to a youth,
A kind of boy, a little scrubbed boy,
No higher than thyself, the judge's clerk.
A prating boy that begg'd it as a fee:
I could not for my heart deny it him.

PORTIA: You were to blame 🠦I must be plain with you
🠦
To part so slightly with your wife's first gift;
A thing stuck on with oaths upon your finger,
And so riveted with faith unto your flesh.
I gave my love a ring and made him swear
Never to part with it: and here he stands;
I dare be sworn for him he would not leave it,
Nor pluck it from his finger, for the wealth
That the world masters. Now, in faith, Gratiano,
You give your wife too unkind a cause of grief:
And 'twere to me, I should be mad at it.
BASSANIO: [*Aside*] Why, I were best to cut my left hand
off,
And swear I lost the ring defending it.

Comment [JB(]: AO3 – The moon was considered 'inconstant' and 'variable' (see

Comment [JB(]: AO1 – Gratiano makes light of his wife's allegation, by simply

Comment [JB(]: AO1 – The dramatic irony is emphasised by Portia's comment

Comment [JB(]: AO1 – Gratiano's disparaging remark about the ring simply

Comment [JB(]: AO2 – Rings are used symbolically throughout the play and are

Comment [JB(]: AO2 – The use of the simile, which compares the inscription on

Comment [JB(]: AO1 – Gratiano quotes the lines that were on the ring, making

Comment [JB(]: AO2 – Nerissa's rhetorical question makes her appear

Comment [JB(]: AO2 – Shakespeare uses dramatic irony here to exploit the

Comment [JB(]: AO1 – Gratiano continues to act arrogantly, assuming that the 'clerk' will become a man. Dramatic irony again increases the humour.

Comment [JB(]: AO1 – Nerissa gives Gratiano another hint that the clerk was,

Comment [JB(]: AO1 – Gratiano's speech adds more comedy, as he

Comment [JB(]: AO2 – The word 'heart' is used ironically here, as Gratiano has

Comment [JB(]: AO1 – Portia's seriousness interrupts the flow of comic

Comment [JB(]: AO2 – The use of metaphors, 'stuck' and 'riveted', make the

Comment [JB(]: AO2 – The use of hyperbole adds still more comedy and

Comment [JB(]: AO1 – Portia is making Bassanio feel more and more

Comment [JB(]: AO1 – Bassanio is so afraid of Portia's reaction, he is

#8

AQA-style Specimen Assessment Material 8: The Merchant of Venice
Read the following extract from Act 5 Scene 1 of *The Merchant of Venice* and then answer the question that follows.

Starting with this speech, explore how Shakespeare presents Lorenzo and Jessica.
Write about:
• how Shakespeare presents the relationship between Lorenzo and Jessica in the extract.
• how Shakespeare presents the relationship between Lorenzo and Jessica in the play as a whole.

At this point in the play, Lorenzo and Jessica are enjoying the moonlit garden in Belmont. This extract is important because Shakespeare seems to question the nature of real love with the references to famous and infamous lovers from myth and literature.

EXTRACT

Enter Musicians

LORENZO
Come, ho! and wake Diana with a hymn!
With sweetest touches pierce your mistress' ear,
And draw her home with music.

Music

JESSICA
I am never merry when I hear sweet music.

LORENZO
The reason is, your spirits are attentive:
For do but note a wild and wanton herd,
Or race of youthful and unhandled colts,
Fetching mad bounds, bellowing and neighing loud,
Which is the hot condition of their blood;
If they but hear perchance a trumpet sound,
Or any air of music touch their ears,

Comment [JB(]: AO3 – The reference to the Roman goddess of the moon does not necessarily augur well for Lorenzo's relationship with Jessica. The moon was considered 'inconstant' and 'variable' (see Juliet's speech in Romeo and Juliet 2.1 [1591-5])

Comment [JB(]: AO1 – Lorenzo is trying to improve Jessica's mood, as she may have become upset earlier in the scene when he described her as a 'shrew', or a bad-tempered aggressively assertive woman.

Comment [JB(]: AO2 – Jessica's speech uses hyperbole to emphasise how little chance there is that 'sweet music' will improve her mood.

Comment [JB(]: AO1 – Lorenzo continue to compliment Jessica and her spiritual awareness, presumably in the hope that she will respond positively. On the other hand, he may be being facetious, as music is generally thought to be capable of uplifting the spirit. Thus far, there is no response to his attempts to improve her mood.
AO2 – The use of personification of Jessica's 'spirits' exaggerates their importance and the word 'attentive' makes them seem too precise to actually be spirits. Spirits are normally associated with freedom more than meticulousness.

You shall perceive them make a mutual stand,
Their savage eyes turn'd to a modest gaze
By the sweet power of music: therefore the poet
Did feign that Orpheus drew trees, stones and floods;
Since nought so stockish, hard and full of rage,
But music for the time doth change his nature.
The man that hath no music in himself,
Nor is not moved with concord of sweet sounds,
Is fit for treasons, stratagems and spoils;
The motions of his spirit are dull as night
And his affections dark as Erebus:
Let no such man be trusted. Mark the music.

Comment [JB(]: AO1 – Lorenzo states that young, male horses are much more likely to respond to music. This reference implies physicality and sexuality, which in

Comment [JB(]: AO2 – Lorenzo uses a tricolon to emphasise how music can be moving. Inanimate objects like 'trees' and 'stones' can be moved, so that begs the

Comment [JB(]: AO2 – Lorenzo's speech contains another tricolon, which emphasises the transformative quality of music. By resisting its power, Jessica

Comment [JB(]: AO2 – This figure of speech seems to refer to the lack of harmony in Lorenzo's relationship with Jessica.

Comment [JB(]: AO2 – Another tricolon in Lorenzo's speech highlights the idea that someone unmoved by music must be a scheming and treasonous robber.

Comment [JB(]: AO2 – This simile is quite odd as juxtaposes 'night' with dullness, instead of romantic excitement, which is what it is normally associated

Comment [JB(]: AO2 – Another negative simile, suggesting that someone who cannot be moved by music must possess emotions that belong in hell, does not

Comment [JB(]: AO1 – Lorenzo ends his speech with a command, telling his wife to listen to the music.
AO2 – The use of the alliterative 'm'

Comment [JB(]: AO3 – This Biblical references alludes to how Jacob managed to get paid in lambs for looking after his uncle's sheep. Shakespeare shows how

Comment [JB(]: AO1 – Shylock uses the word 'holy' to show his respect to his own religion, Judaism, which hold Abram to be main person responsible for the special

Comment [JB(]: AO1 – Antonio interrupts Shylock's story with a couple of direct questions. He appears to be becoming impatient with his Biblical

#9

AQA-style Specimen Assessment Material 9: The Merchant of Venice
Read the following extract from Act 1 Scene 3 of *The Merchant of Venice* and then answer the question that follows.

Starting with this speech, explore how Shakespeare presents the theme of religion.
Write about:
• how Shakespeare presents the theme of religion in the extract.
• how Shakespeare presents the theme of religion in the play as a whole.

At this point in the play, Antonio is asking to borrow three thousand ducats for three months. Shylock is considering whether he should grant the loan. This extract is important because Shylock uses religion to justify charging interest.

EXTRACT

SHYLOCK
When Jacob grazed his uncle Laban's sheep--
This Jacob from our holy Abram was,
As his wise mother wrought in his behalf,
The third possessor; ay, he was the third--

ANTONIO
And what of him? did he take interest?

SHYLOCK

No, not take interest, not, as you would say,
Directly interest: mark what Jacob did:
When Laban and himself were compromised
That all the eanlings which were streak'd and pied
Should fall as Jacob's hire, the ewes, being rank,
In the end of autumn turned to the rams,
And, when the work of generation was
Between these woolly breeders in the act,
The skilful shepherd peel'd me certain wands,
And, in the doing of the deed of kind,
He stuck them up before the fulsome ewes,
Who then conceiving did in eaning time
Fall parti-colour'd lambs, and those were Jacob's.
This was a way to thrive, and he was blest:
And thrift is blessing, if men steal it not.

ANTONIO
This was a venture, sir, that Jacob served for;
A thing not in his power to bring to pass,
But sway'd and fashion'd by the hand of heaven.
Was this inserted to make interest good?
Or is your gold and silver ewes and rams?

SHYLOCK
I cannot tell; I make it breed as fast:
But note me, signior.

ANTONIO
Mark you this, Bassanio,
The devil can cite Scripture for his purpose.

Comment [JB(]: AO1 – Shylock's enthusiasm to tell his story results a long-winded account of how Jacob made a fence of branches, which the ewes would see, to make the new-born lambs come out 'streak'd and pied'. This would mean that Jacob could keep them, as payment for his services. This shows how Shylock is keen to show off his religious knowledge, particularly when it justifies charging

Comment [JB(]: AO2 – The use of repetition of 'blest' and 'blessing' reminds the audience that Shylock sees himself as a righteous man. The sibilance of 'thrift' and 'thrive' connects these two concepts, making them seem one and the same to Shylock, at least. He makes a virtue out of being careful with money.

Comment [JB(]: AO1 – Antonio seems to lose pateience with this religious story, as he can see tha Shylock is only using to justify charging interest.
AO2 – Antonio uses a rhetorical question at the end of his speech, possibly, to emphasise how inappropriate it is to borrow Biblical stories to justify financial gain.

Comment [JB(]: AO1 – Money appears to be a form of religion to Shylock, who can 'make it breed as fast' as sheep.
AO2 – Shylock uses a simile of reproduction, which makes religion and money tie in more closely with family. This is foreshadowing, given that his daughter, Jessica, will take his money and leave his religion behind her, later in the play.

Comment [JB(]: AO1 – Antonio describes Shylock as 'the devil' who can use the Bible for his own devices, yet he still agrees to make a pact with him. In a sense, Antonio cannot complain that the forfeit is incredibly harsh.

#10

AQA-style Specimen Assessment Material 10: The Merchant of Venice
Read the following extract from Act 3 Scene 1 of *The Merchant of Venice* and then answer the question that follows.

Starting with this speech, explore how Shakespeare presents the theme of revenge.
Write about:
• how Shakespeare presents the theme of revenge in the extract.
• how Shakespeare presents the theme of revenge in the play as a whole.

At this point in the play, Solanio and Salarino have been discussing the news of Antonio's misfortunes at sea and

now that have asked Shylock if he has heard anything about the latter's merchant shipping. This extract is important because the aggrieved Shylock explains what is fuelling his desire for revenge.

EXTRACT

SALARINO: But tell us, do you hear whether Antonio have had any loss at sea or no?

SHYLOCK: There I have another bad match: a bankrupt, a prodigal, who dare scarce show his head on the Rialto; a beggar, that was used to come so smug upon the mart; let him look to his bond: he was wont to call me usurer; let him look to his bond: he was wont to lend money for a Christian courtesy; let him look to his bond.

SALARINO: Why, I am sure, if he forfeit, thou wilt not take his flesh: what's that good for?

SHYLOCK: To bait fish withal: if it will feed nothing else, it will feed my revenge. He hath disgraced me, and hindered me half a million; laughed at my losses, mocked at my gains, scorned my nation, thwarted my bargains, cooled my friends, heated mine enemies; and what's his reason? I am a Jew. Hath not a Jew eyes? hath not a Jew hands, organs, dimensions, senses, affections, passions? fed with the same food, hurt with the same weapons, subject to the same diseases, healed by the same means, warmed and cooled by the same winter and summer, as a Christian is? If you prick us, do we not bleed? if you tickle us, do we not laugh? if you poison us, do we not die? and if you wrong us, shall we not revenge? If we are like you in the rest, we will resemble you in that. If a Jew wrong a Christian, what is his humility? Revenge. If a Christian wrong a Jew, what should his sufferance be by Christian example? Why, revenge. The villany you teach me, I will execute, and it shall go hard but I will better the instruction.

#11

AQA-style Specimen Assessment Material 11: The Merchant of Venice

Read the following extract from Act 2 Scene 5 of *The Merchant of Venice* and then answer the question that follows.

Comment [JB(]: AO2 – The use of prose instead of verse suggests that the topic of conversation is low rather than elevated.

Comment [JB(]: AO2 – Shylock's speech uses an ascending tricolon to make the description of his contempt for Antonio

Comment [JB(]: AO1 – If Antonio was indeed smug, it is understandable that Shylock became resentful of such a

Comment [JB(]: AO2 – The anaphora of 'he was wont to' powerfully emphasises how different Antonio is to Shylock, who

Comment [JB(]: AO2 – This phrase is repeated three times for effect. It shows that Shylock is unlikely to be merciful.

Comment [JB(]: AO2 – Salarino uses a rhetorical question to attempt to bring Shylock to his senses, as he cannot see

Comment [JB(]: AO3 – The fish is a symbol of Christianity as, in the New Testament, Jesus fed five thousand

Comment [JB(]: AO1 – Answering Salarino's rhetorical question, Shylock says he'll use Antonio's flesh as fish bait.

Comment [JB(]: AO3 – Shylock's thirst for revenge makes the play generically mixed, despite its comic elements. While

Comment [JB(]: AO2 – The personification of revenge as a feeding animal makes it appear all the more

Comment [JB(]: AO2 – Shylock's lists all injustices that he has suffered and believes that Antonio is responsible for.

Comment [JB(]: AO2 – Shylock's speech uses a rhetorical question to add impact to the answer. It emphasises that the sole

Comment [JB(]: AO2 – A series of rhetorical questions follow which makes this speech incredibly powerful.

Comment [JB(]: AO1 – The answer to all the rhetorical questions is revenge. AO2 – 'Revenge' is repeated three times,

Comment [JB(]: AO1 – Shylock claims that he has been taught 'villany' by the Christians and is threatening to wreak

Starting with this speech, explore how Shakespeare presents the theme of greed and gluttony.
Write about:
• how Shakespeare presents the theme of greed and gluttony in the extract.
• how Shakespeare presents the theme of greed and gluttony in the play as a whole.

At this point in the play, Shylock is calling Jessica to let her know that he has been invited to dinner by Bassanio. This extract is important because it is the first time that we can see Shylock at home, so we can develop a deeper understanding of his character through his relationships with his daughter, Jessica, and his servant, Lancelot.

EXTRACT

SHYLOCK
I am bid forth to supper, Jessica:
There are my keys. But wherefore should I go?
I am not bid for love; they flatter me:
But yet I'll go in hate, to feed upon
The prodigal Christian. Jessica, my girl,
Look to my house. I am right loath to go:
There is some ill a-brewing towards my rest,
For I did dream of money-bags to-night.

LAUNCELOT
I beseech you, sir, go: my young master doth expect your reproach.

SHYLOCK
So do I his.

LAUNCELOT
An they have conspired together, I will not say you shall see a masque; but if you do, then it was not for nothing that my nose fell a-bleeding on Black-Monday last at six o'clock i' the morning, falling out that year on Ash-Wednesday was four year, in the afternoon.

SHYLOCK
What, are there masques? Hear you me, Jessica:
Lock up my doors; and when you hear the drum
And the vile squealing of the wry-neck'd fife,
Clamber not you up to the casements then,
Nor thrust your head into the public street
To gaze on Christian fools with varnish'd faces,

Comment [JB(]: AO2 – Shylock uses a rhetorical question, as he wonders why he should eat with people that do not like him. However, he has already seemingly decided that he is going, perhaps to eat their food. A sense of greed or gluttony

Comment [JB(]: AO1 – Shylock makes it clear that he understands that the Christians 'flatter' him because he is granting Antonio a loan. Shylock's 'hate' for the Christians is stated, but he is ready 'to feed upon' them and benefit from

Comment [JB(]: AO3 – In Shakespeare's time, dreaming of 'money-bags' signified loss of money, whereas nowadays this imagery would viewed as an example of Shylock's vision of accumulating wealth. However, rather than representing the

Comment [JB(]: AO2 – Shakespeare's use of a malapropism (the word 'reproach' meaning 'approach') for Launcelot's speech makes it seem as if Bassanio expects Shylock's disapproval rather than his arrival. This adds humour

Comment [JB(]: AO3 – This could be a reference to a historical event, which occurred on Easter Monday, 14th April 1360. On that fateful day, many of Edward III's army died because it was so bitterly cold. The juxtaposition of the day

Comment [JB(]: AO3 – Ash Wednesday is in the Christian calendar and is set aside as a day to fast, abstain and repent. It ironic that Launcelot is mentioning it here as the last time he had a nose bleed, as Shylock's intention is to 'feed upon the

Comment [JB(]: AO2 – Shylock uses a rhetorical question to show a sense of shock at the idea that there may be masques going on.
AO3 – Masques were a popular form of entertainment in the sixteenth century.

Comment [JB(]: AO1 – Shylock commands Jessica to steer clear of the revelry and festivities of the Carnival of Venice, where greed and gluttony, amongst other sins, will be indulged in before the commencement of the

But stop my house's ears, I mean my casements:
Let not the sound of shallow foppery enter
My sober house. By Jacob's staff, I swear,
I have no mind of feasting forth to-night:
But I will go. Go you before me, sirrah;
Say I will come.

#12

AQA-style Specimen Assessment Material 12: The Merchant of Venice
Read the following extract from Act 4 Scene 1 of *The Merchant of Venice* and then answer the question that follows.

Starting with this speech, explore how Shakespeare presents the theme of mercy.
Write about:
• how Shakespeare presents the theme of mercy in the extract.
• how Shakespeare presents the theme of mercy in the play as a whole.

At this point in the play, Portia (disguised as Doctor Balthazar) tries to persuade Shylock to be merciful and not to punish Antonio too severely. This extract is important because, in disguise, it is easier for Portia to impose her views on the court. Appearing to the other characters as a male doctor of law, she is regarded as an esteemed professional to be respected and taken seriously.

EXTRACT

PORTIA
The quality of mercy is not strain'd,
It droppeth as the gentle rain from heaven
Upon the place beneath: it is twice blest;
It blesseth him that gives and him that takes:
'Tis mightiest in the mightiest: it becomes
The throned monarch better than his crown;
His sceptre shows the force of temporal power,
The attribute to awe and majesty,
Wherein doth sit the dread and fear of kings;
But mercy is above this sceptred sway;
It is enthroned in the hearts of kings,
It is an attribute to God himself;

Comment [JB(]: AO2 – Shylock uses negative language to remind Jessica not to take part in in the masque. He uses the words 'not' and 'nor', as well as the word 'stop' to instruct her how to behave while

Comment [JB(]: AO1 – Shylock describes the festivities as 'shallow foppery' which means hollow nonsense, but his greed and gluttony are still going to take him into the midst of the carnival.

Comment [JB(]: AO3 – Although this sounds like a Biblical reference, it actually refers to an early form of sextant, which makes it more nautical than religious imagery. It is interesting that Shylock is

Comment [JB(]: AO1 – Shylock denies that greed or gluttony is the reason for his visit, yet has decided he will go anyway. It is difficult to determine what exactly is motivating him.

Comment [JB(]: AO3 – Mercy is a virtue in many faiths, including Judaism and Christianity so, by appealing to this quality, Portia is exploring common ground between to the two faiths.

Comment [JB(]: AO1 – Portia's gentle approach hinges on appealing to Shylock's better nature. By reminding him that 'mercy is not strain'd', she is saying that it cannot be forced. She is giving Shylock

Comment [JB(]: AO2 – Portia's speech personifies mercy as 'gentle rain from heaven', which gives it a holy quality. Again, Portia is exploring the common belief in heaven held by both faiths.

Comment [JB(]: AO2 – A form of repetition is used here to make Portia's speech more persuasive, when 'blest' becomes 'blesseth'. This emphasises how highly regarded the attribute of mercy is.

Comment [JB(]: AO2 – The repeated use of the superlative 'mightiest' is persuasive as it informs Shylock that the more merciful you are, the more powerful you are as person.

Comment [JB(]: AO2 – The personification of mercy as 'enthroned in the hearts of kings' makes it appear to be a ruler living inside the most virtuous of monarchs. Again, Portia's argument is the

And earthly power doth then show likest God's
When mercy seasons justice. Therefore, Jew,
Though justice be thy plea, consider this,
That, in the course of justice, none of us
Should see salvation: we do pray for mercy;
And that same prayer doth teach us all to render
The deeds of mercy. I have spoke thus much
To mitigate the justice of thy plea;
Which if thou follow, this strict court of Venice
Must needs give sentence 'gainst the merchant there.

#13

AQA-style Specimen Assessment Material 13: The Merchant of Venice
Read the following extract from Act 4 Scene 1 of *The Merchant of Venice* and then answer the question that follows.

Starting with this speech, explore how Shakespeare presents the theme of loss.
Write about:
• how Shakespeare presents the theme of loss in the extract.
• how Shakespeare presents the theme of loss in the play as a whole.

At this point in the play, Antonio has the opportunity to deliver what he thinks will be his last words, before facing almost certain death at the hands of Shylock, who is still insisting on removing a pound of flesh. This extract is important because, facing death, it is easier for Antonio to express himself freely, as any ramifications from his words will resonate after his punishment is complete.

EXTRACT

ANTONIO
But little; I am arm'd and well prepared.
Give me your hand, Bassanio: fare you well!
Grieve not that I am fallen to this for you;
For herein Fortune shows herself more kind
Than is her custom: it is still her use
To let the wretched man outlive his wealth,
To view with hollow eye and wrinkled brow
An age of poverty; from which lingering penance

Comment [JB(]: AO1 – Although Portia has already mentioned that mercy is 'above' a monarch's sceptre, in terms of power, she has now stated that even God would consider mercy an 'attribute'. She

Comment [JB(]: AO2 – Portia's speech uses sibilance in the phrase 'should see salvation' to emphasise how important it is that our souls are saved and elevated to heaven after death.

Comment [JB(]: AO2 – Inclusive language, through the use of the first-person plural pronoun 'we', emphasises the idea that humanity is united and the same. It is persuasive and convincing.

Comment [JB(]: AO1 – Portia admits she has spoken at length about mercy and concludes by stating that her intention is to soften the punishment that Antonio will receive.

Comment [JB(]: AO1 – Antonio's says he has 'little' to say but he is remaining defiant, knowing he will lose a pound of flesh and, almost definitely, his life.

Comment [JB(]: AO2 – The largely iambic rhythm is broken by the word 'fallen', which draws attention to it. This adds to the tragedy of the situation, as a man who has reached great heights has

Comment [JB(]: AO3 – Many Elizabethans (those that were not 'humanists') believed in a wheel of fortune, which was the main controlling force in life. Antonio has little choice but

Comment [JB(]: AO2 – A regular line of iambic pentameter adds to the sense that Antonio is bravely accepting his fate, describing it as 'kind'. He is accepting his loss with honour.

Comment [JB(]: AO2 – The use of graphic imagery such as 'hollow eye and wrinkled brow' portrays the negative side of growing older. Clearly, Antonio is trying to play down the loss of life that he faces.

Comment [JB(]: AO1 – Antonio appears to be persuading himself that it is better to die relatively young than it is to cling onto life to become poverty-stricken in one's latter years.

Of such misery doth she cut me off.
Commend me to your honourable wife:
Tell her the process of Antonio's end;
Say how I loved you, speak me fair in death;
And, when the tale is told, bid her be judge
Whether Bassanio had not once a love.
Repent but you that you shall lose your friend,
And he repents not that he pays your debt;
For if the Jew do cut but deep enough,
I'll pay it presently with all my heart.

#14

AQA-style Specimen Assessment Material 14: The Merchant of Venice
Read the following extract from Act 4 Scene 1 of *The Merchant of Venice* and then answer the question that follows.

Starting with this speech, explore how Shakespeare presents the theme of justice and the law.
Write about:
• how Shakespeare presents the theme of justice and the law in the extract.
• how Shakespeare presents the theme of justice and the law as a whole.

At this point in the play, Shylock is appearing in the Duke's palace in Venice, which is the court for the trial of Antonio. This extract is important because the audience can hear how Shylock formally expresses his grievances against the defendant, Antonio, as the play nears its climax.

EXTRACT

SHYLOCK
I have possess'd your grace of what I purpose;
And by our holy Sabbath have I sworn
To have the due and forfeit of my bond:
If you deny it, let the danger light
Upon your charter and your city's freedom.
You'll ask me, why I rather choose to have
A weight of carrion flesh than to receive
Three thousand ducats: I'll not answer that:
But, say, it is my humour: is it answer'd?
What if my house be troubled with a rat

Comment [JB(]: AO3 – The imminent death of Antonio mirrors what happens in Ser Giovanni's 'Il Pecorone' (published in 1558), where Ansaldo is saved from 'a Jew of Mestri' who insists on a pound of

Comment [JB(]: AO1 – Antonio's primary concern is more about how he will be spoken of after the imminent loss of his life, which he is bravely facing up to.

Comment [JB(]: AO2 – The use of alliteration heightens the tragic idea that soon Antonio will lose his life on this earth and he will only exist in stories.

Comment [JB(]: AO2 – The use of iambic pentameter for the last four lines makes the content appear more tragic. The use of the word 'heart' is meant literally and metaphorically here, as if

Comment [JB(]: AO1 – Shylock's determination to have justice is made clear by his insistence that he has sworn on the 'holy Sabbath'.
AO3 – The 'Sabbath' is Saturday in

Comment [JB(]: AO1 – Shylock threatens the Duke, by reminding him of the possible repercussions of not providing the opportunity for justice to be served.

Comment [JB(]: AO2 – The use of iambic pentameter makes this part of Shylock's speech seem particularly serious and weighty. The Duke, therefore, must acknowledge the possible repercussions

Comment [JB(]: AO1 – Shylock has embraced the counter-argument somewhat, when he anticipates that he will be asked why choosing a pound of dead flesh over three thousand ducats

Comment [JB(]: AO2 – Eventually, Shylock uses a rhetorical question to ask the Duke and the court whether or not they are satisfied with his answer. Shylock suggests that it might be his 'humour'

And I be pleased to give ten thousand ducats
To have it baned? What, are you answer'd yet?
Some men there are love not a gaping pig;
Some, that are mad if they behold a cat;
And others, when the bagpipe sings i' the nose,
Cannot contain their urine: for affection,
Mistress of passion, sways it to the mood
Of what it likes or loathes. Now, for your answer:
As there is no firm reason to be render'd,
Why he cannot abide a gaping pig;
Why he, a harmless necessary cat;
Why he, a woollen bagpipe; but of force
Must yield to such inevitable shame
As to offend, himself being offended;
So can I give no reason, nor I will not,
More than a lodged hate and a certain loathing
I bear Antonio, that I follow thus
A losing suit against him. Are you answer'd?

Comment [JB(]: AO2 – The use of an anecdote of a poisoned rat makes Shylock's argument stronger, if we can accept that Antonio is less than a human being. Bearing in mind the inhumane way that Antonio has treated Shylock in the past, it is possible to understand the train of thought.

Comment [JB(]: AO2 – The alliterative 'r' in 'reason to be rendered' sounds like growling, which makes Shylock appear to be dog-like in his tenacity. His anger makes it is understandable that he is insisting on harsh justice.

Comment [JB(]: AO3 – Pigs, which are eaten by Christians, are considered to be disgustingly dirty and off limits by some religious groups, including Jews. Shylock could be using this example to show that you cannot explain the almost inexplicable.

Comment [JB(]: AO1 – Shylock admits he cannot or will not give a reason for continuing this unprofitable pursuit of justice.

Comment [JB(]: AO1 – Shylock ends his speech with a defiant question, which implies that he does not expect justice (perhaps given the prejudice he has endured all his life).

Comment [JB(]: AO1 – Portia refers to Shylock as 'Jew' rather than by his name. It indicates that his religion is more important than his character in sixteenth-century Venice. Therefore, he can only expect harsh punishment in a society that does not treat Jews as equal to Christians.
AO2 – The use of an extremely short sentence makes Portia's command seem abrupt and disrespectful.
AO3 – To call somebody 'Jew' in Elizabethan times would have been considered less rude then than it is today. However, it cannot be considered as respectful either in this context.

#15

AQA-style Specimen Assessment Material 15: The Merchant of Venice
Read the following extract from Act 4 Scene 1 of *The Merchant of Venice* and then answer the question that follows.

Starting with this speech, explore how Shakespeare presents the theme of suffering and punishment.
Write about:
• how Shakespeare presents the theme of suffering and punishment in the extract.
• how Shakespeare presents the theme of suffering and punishment as a whole.

At this point in the play, Portia has revealed a loophole in Shylock's bond, which means he will break the law if Antonio bleeds while losing a pound of flesh. Therefore, Shylock has decided to leave with nothing. This extract is important because the audience may sympathise with Shylock again, given the harsh treatment he receives.

EXTRACT

PORTIA
Tarry, Jew:
The law hath yet another hold on you.

It is enacted in the laws of Venice,
If it be proved against an alien
That by direct or indirect attempts
He seek the life of any citizen,
The party 'gainst the which he doth contrive
Shall seize one half his goods; the other half
Comes to the privy coffer of the state;
And the offender's life lies in the mercy
Of the duke only, 'gainst all other voice.
In which predicament, I say, thou stand'st;
For it appears, by manifest proceeding,
That indirectly and directly too
Thou hast contrived against the very life
Of the defendant; and thou hast incurr'd
The danger formerly by me rehearsed.
Down therefore and beg mercy of the duke.

Comment [JB(): AO2 - The word 'alien' implies that Shylock is not equal to 'any citizen' in the eyes of the law. As a result, he can only expect injustice and suffering in a court of law.

Comment [JB(): AO3 – In sixteenth-century Venice, Jews were confined to living in the ghetto, so in a sense they were already treated like aliens before they were declared as 'enemy aliens' in 1943 by Mussolini's Fascist government.

Comment [JB(): AO1 – Shylock's suffering is increasing all the time, as he learns that half of his wealth should go to Antonio, while the other half will be absorbed by the state.

Comment [JB(): AO2 – The use of legal language makes Portia's speech appear more authoritative and convincing. The Duke's 'privy coffer' stands to increase as the result of the seizure of half of Shylock's wealth. Therefore, it is in the interests of the Duke to increase Shylock's suffering.

Comment [JB(): AO1 – Portia advises Shylock to get down on his hands and knees, so he can for beg the Duke's mercy. Shylock is suffering in a different way to previously, as he is now having to hope the Duke shows mercy.

#16

AQA-style Specimen Assessment Material 16: The Merchant of Venice
Read the following extract from Act 2 Scene 2 of *The Merchant of Venice* and then answer the question that follows.

Starting with this speech, explore how Shakespeare presents the theme of disloyalty and betrayal.
Write about:
• how Shakespeare presents the theme of disloyalty and betrayal in the extract.
• how Shakespeare presents the theme of disloyalty and betrayal as a whole.

At this point in the play, Bassanio has just entered the scene near Shylock's house, where Lancelot is complaining to his father about his job as Shylock's servant and how he is intending to run away. Gobbo (the father) introduces his son to Bassanio. This extract is important because the audience can begin to decide whether Lancelot's disloyalty is justified.

EXTRACT

GOBBO
Here's my son, sir, a poor boy,--

LAUNCELOT

Not a poor boy, sir, but the rich Jew's man; that would, sir, as my father shall specify--

GOBBO
He hath a great infection, sir, as one would say, to serve--

LAUNCELOT
Indeed, the short and the long is, I serve the Jew, and have a desire, as my father shall specify--

GOBBO
His master and he, saving your worship's reverence, are scarce cater-cousins--

LAUNCELOT
To be brief, the very truth is that the Jew, having done me wrong, doth cause me, as my father, being, I hope, an old man, shall frutify unto you--

GOBBO
I have here a dish of doves that I would bestow upon your worship, and my suit is--

LAUNCELOT
In very brief, the suit is impertinent to myself, as your worship shall know by this honest old man; and, though I say it, though old man, yet poor man, my father.

BASSANIO
One speak for both. What would you?

LAUNCELOT
Serve you, sir.

GOBBO
That is the very defect of the matter, sir.

BASSANIO
I know thee well; thou hast obtain'd thy suit:
Shylock thy master spoke with me this day,
And hath preferr'd thee, if it be preferment
To leave a rich Jew's service, to become
The follower of so poor a gentleman.

LAUNCELOT
The old proverb is very well parted between my master Shylock and you, sir: you have the grace of God, sir, and he hath enough.

#17

AQA-style Specimen Assessment Material 17: The Merchant

Comment [JB(]: AO1 – Lancelot immediately contradicts his father, as he is trying to make a good impression on his prospective employer.
AO2 – The fact that he describes himself as 'the rich Jew's man' makes it sound like he should have a sense of belonging, as the description suggests possession. However, his failure to name Shylock makes it appear as if he has little or no respect for his master, making Lancelot appear disloyal.

Comment [JB(]: AO2 – Gobbo's malapropisms makes Lancelot's attempt at securing new employment (and consequent betrayal of Shylock) comic to the audience. Gobbo means 'affection' rather than 'infection', of course.

Comment [JB(]: AO2 – Lancelot is no better at stating his case, which adds to the comic effect, as instead of saying 'the long and short of it is', he reverses the natural collocation.

Comment [JB(]: AO1 – Gobbo reveals that his son is not exactly friends with his current employer, which makes Lancelot appear disloyal.

Comment [JB(]: AO1 – Although Lancelot claims that Shylock has wronged him, he has not specified what has been done to him. Therefore, the audience, while seeing Lancelot as an amusing

Comment [JB(]: AO1 – Bassanio asks for just one of them to act as a spokesman. In a sense, this implies that disloyalty is two-faced, as it literally has two voices here.

Comment [JB(]: AO1 – Shylock appears to be more loyal than Lancelot, as he has actually recommended him to Bassanio.

Comment [JB(]: AO3 – The prejudice against Jews is evident here, as Lancelot would prefer to work for a poor Christian.

Comment [JB(]: AO3 – The original proverb is: 'The grace of God is gear [wealth] enough'. The obsessive pursuit of money is regarded as anathema to Christians, which may be why Lancelot

of Venice

Read the following extract from Act 3 Scene 2 of *The Merchant of Venice* and then answer the question that follows.

Starting with this speech, explore how Shakespeare presents the role and power of women.
Write about:
• how Shakespeare presents the role and power of women in the extract.
• how Shakespeare presents the role and power of women as a whole.

At this point in the play, Bassanio, Portia, Nerissa, Gratiano and all their trains have entered Portia's great hall ahead of the casket test. This extract is important because the audience can witness another side to Portia's character, which is warmer and less aloof than we have seen with other suitors.

EXTRACT

PORTIA

Away, then! I am lock'd in one of them:
If you do love me, you will find me out.
Nerissa and the rest, stand all aloof.
Let music sound while he doth make his choice;
Then, if he lose, he makes a swan-like end,
Fading in music: that the comparison
May stand more proper, my eye shall be the stream
And watery death-bed for him. He may win;
And what is music then? Then music is
Even as the flourish when true subjects bow
To a new-crowned monarch: such it is
As are those dulcet sounds in break of day
That creep into the dreaming bridegroom's ear,
And summon him to marriage. Now he goes,
With no less presence, but with much more love,
Than young Alcides, when he did redeem
The virgin tribute paid by howling Troy
To the sea-monster: I stand for sacrifice
The rest aloof are the Dardanian wives,
With bleared visages, come forth to view
The issue of the exploit. Go, Hercules!
Live thou, I live: with much, much more dismay

Comment [JB(]: AO2 – The metaphor 'lock'd' tells us that Portia lacks freedom of choice. Clearly, she would choose Bassanio, if she could, but he is subject to the same 'lottery' as the rest of her

Comment [JB(]: AO1 – By using the phrase 'if you love me', Portia expresses some doubt about Bassanio's devotion to her. Her lack of power in society is evidenced by the fact that she has to

Comment [JB(]: AO1 – The addition of music to the scene enhances the romance and drama of the scene. Subtly, Portia is voicing her to desire to see Bassanio succeed.

Comment [JB(]: AO2 – The bird imagery makes Bassanio appear to be pure of heart, as a swan's white feathers can be linked to purity. This description adds drama and makes her seem like a

Comment [JB(]: AO2 – the use of the extended metaphor of the dying swan swimming in her tears, makes this moment all the more poignant. Portia is powerless to intervene, yet has the power

Comment [JB(]: AO2 – Two lines of iambic pentameter add weight to Portia's message that sound is important. Perhaps she subtly hinting to Bassanio that 'lead' sounds like 'led' and that choosing the

Comment [JB(]: AO1 – Portia contradicts herself here, as earlier she expressed some doubts about Bassanio's love by using the word 'if'. Now she appears more certain, as she claims

Comment [JB(]: AO1 – Portia appears to see herself as a helpless victim, as she refers to herself as a 'sacrifice' to 'the sea monster' at the gates of Troy. Only Hercules can save her.

Comment [JB(]: AO1 – One of the only powers that Portia has in this scene is to add to the drama by describing the moment in mythological terms. She now describes the other characters present at

I view the fight than thou that makest the fray.

#18

AQA-style Specimen Assessment Material 18: The Merchant of Venice
Read the following extract from Act 2 Scene 7 of *The Merchant of Venice* and then answer the question that follows.

Starting with this speech, explore how Shakespeare presents the theme of appearances versus reality.
Write about:
• how Shakespeare presents the theme of appearances versus reality in the extract.
• how Shakespeare presents the theme of appearances versus reality as a whole.

At this point in the play, Portia, the Prince of Morocco and both their trains have entered a room in Portia's house ahead of the casket test. This extract is important because the audience can witness how appearances can be deceptive.

EXTRACT

MOROCCO
Let's see once more this saying graved in gold
'Who chooseth me shall gain what many men desire.'
Why, that's the lady; all the world desires her;
From the four corners of the earth they come,
To kiss this shrine, this mortal-breathing saint:
The Hyrcanian deserts and the vasty wilds
Of wide Arabia are as thoroughfares now
For princes to come view fair Portia:
The watery kingdom, whose ambitious head
Spits in the face of heaven, is no bar
To stop the foreign spirits, but they come,
As o'er a brook, to see fair Portia.
One of these three contains her heavenly picture.
Is't like that lead contains her? 'Twere damnation
To think so base a thought: it were too gross
To rib her cerecloth in the obscure grave.
Or shall I think in silver she's immured,
Being ten times undervalued to tried gold?
O sinful thought! Never so rich a gem
Was set in worse than gold. They have in England

Comment [JB(]: AO1 – Portia assumes that she is more anxious than Bassanio, at this moment. If he does not win the 'lottery' of the casket test, she may be forced to marry someone much less desirable, so it highlights her powerlessness.

Comment [JB(]: AO2 – The alliteration of 'graved in gold' emphasises these words and although 'graved' literally means engraved, it could also connote death if one associates it with graves.

Comment [JB(]: AO1 – This inscription is misleading, as the young suitor is unlikely to guess that 'many men desire' death. The cold reality is hidden by the tempting words.

Comment [JB(]: AO1 – Morocco jumps to the erroneous conclusion that 'the lady' is what 'many men desire'. He has been deceived by appearances.

Comment [JB(]: AO2 – Morocco uses a simile to show how the sea or 'watery kingdom' is only the size of 'a brook' to those suitors that have travelled 'from the four corner of the earth' to try their luck.

Comment [JB(]: AO3 – Lead was used during the Elizabethan era as a beauty product. Queen Elizabeth herself was noted for her pale skin, like 'fair Portia', and would have used 'ceruse', which was

Comment [JB(]: AO1 – Morocco cannot consider the lead casket, as he is predisposed to believe that it is 'base' and 'too gross' a metal to even enclose a corpse. He is making decisions based on

Comment [JB(]: AO1 – Morocco rules out the silver casket, stating that it is worth 'ten times' less than gold. In effect, he is making ineffectual comparison, as he has been lured by beautiful

Comment [JB(]: AO2 – The metaphor of 'a gem' is used to describe Portia here. This reminds us that she is 'richly-left', so the winner of the casket test stands to make a fortune. Perhaps she appears to

A coin that bears the figure of an angel
Stamped in gold, but that's insculp'd upon;
But here an angel in a golden bed
Lies all within. Deliver me the key:
Here do I choose, and thrive I as I may!

PORTIA
There, take it, prince; and if my form lie there,
Then I am yours.

He unlocks the golden casket

Comment [JB(]: AO3 – Morocco appears to be referring to an Elizabethan coin that was known as an 'angel'. While it was worth double a Venetian ducat or an English crown (the most commonly used coin), a lot of these coins were in circulation and were only worth half a pound. Therefore, Morocco seems to be fooling himself about the value of the gold casket.

Comment [JB(]: AO1 – Morocco deceives himself with the power of his own imagination, as he visualises an 'angel in a golden bed'.
AO2 – The metaphor of 'an angel' makes Portia appear heavenly, when the reality is she wishes him 'A gentle riddance' and does not wish him to succeed.

#19

AQA-style Specimen Assessment Material 19: The Merchant of Venice
Read the following extract from Act 4 Scene 1 of *The Merchant of Venice* and then answer the question that follows.

Starting with this speech, explore how Shakespeare presents the theme of prejudice.
Write about:
• how Shakespeare presents the theme of prejudice in the extract.
• how Shakespeare presents the theme of prejudice as a whole.

At this point in the play, Shylock is getting ready to extract a pound of flesh from Antonio, who appears to be doomed. This extract is important because the audience can witness how insidious anti-Semitism rears its ugly head, especially at a time of heightened drama.

EXTRACT

BASSANIO
Why dost thou whet thy knife so earnestly?

SHYLOCK
To cut the forfeiture from that bankrupt there.

GRATIANO
Not on thy sole, but on thy soul, harsh Jew,

Comment [JB(]: AO1 – Shylock's answer to Bassanio's question ignites the verbal invective that follows. The use of the word 'bankrupt', while truly describing Antonio, is harsh and dismissive. Therefore, it works dramatically to provoke Gratiano.

Comment [JB(]: AO2 – The use of the homophones 'sole' and 'soul' make the puns in Gratiano's speech equate Shylock's spiritual side with something that he may have stepped on.
AO3 – The Elizabethan belief in heaven and hell would have meant that the audience would expect Shlock's soul to be eternally damned if he went through with his threat to cut a pound of Antonio's flesh. Additionally, his faith might also have seen him rejected at the gates of heaven.

Thou makest thy knife keen; but no metal can,
No, not the hangman's axe, bear half the keenness
Of thy sharp envy. Can no prayers pierce thee?

SHYLOCK
No, none that thou hast wit enough to make.

GRATIANO
O, be thou damn'd, inexecrable dog!
And for thy life let justice be accused.
Thou almost makest me waver in my faith
To hold opinion with Pythagoras,
That souls of animals infuse themselves
Into the trunks of men: thy currish spirit
Govern'd a wolf, who, hang'd for human slaughter,
Even from the gallows did his fell soul fleet,
And, whilst thou lay'st in thy unhallow'd dam,
Infused itself in thee; for thy desires
Are wolvish, bloody, starved and ravenous.

#20

AQA-style Specimen Assessment Material 20: The Merchant of Venice
Read the following extract from Act 2 Scene 9 of *The Merchant of Venice* and then answer the question that follows.

Starting with this speech, explore how Shakespeare presents the themes of arrogance, pride and over-confidence.
Write about:
• how Shakespeare presents the themes of arrogance, pride and over-confidence in the extract.
• how Shakespeare presents the theme of arrogance, pride and over-confidence as a whole.

At this point in the play, the Prince of Arragon has arrived with his train and Portia, in a room at Belmont, to take the casket test. This extract is important because the audience can witness how pride comes before a fall, or two fool's heads, in this case.

EXTRACT

ARRAGON
And so have I address'd me. Fortune now
To my heart's hope! Gold; silver; and base lead.

Comment [JB(]: AO1 – The personification of 'envy' as 'sharp' makes it seem as if Shylock's presumed jealousy of Antonio's position is the motivating force. In fact, much of the text seems to indicate that Shylock's motivation for revenge is more likely to be the ill-treatment and prejudice he has long suffered at the hands of Antonio.

Comment [JB(]: AO2 – Gratiano's rhetorical question here is a call of desperation, rather than a serious attempt to stop Shylock, who seems resolute.
AO3 – Of course, Gratiano is well aware

Comment [JB(]: AO1 – Shylock replies to the rhetorical question, by questioning Gratiano's 'wit' or intelligence.
AO2 – This is important, structurally, as it sparks Gratiano's outraged and prejudiced response.

Comment [JB(]: AO2 – Structurally, the exclamation mark shows the vehemence of Gratiano's angry response. Meanwhile, Shylock is once again referred to as a dog, which implies he lacks the status of a Christian and is, instead, down at heel.

Comment [JB(]: AO3 – Gratiano invokes the work of the Greek philosopher who believed that after death, a human soul could pass into another being. He is trying to justify comparing Shylock to a dog and other animals.

Comment [JB(]: AO2 – Calling Shylock's mother an unholy female animal is particularly insulting and dehumanising. This reveals Gratiano's prejudice.

Comment [JB(]: AO2 – The use of a tetracolon brings the insulting, prejudicial language to a crescendo. The animalistic imagery shows that Gratiano views Shylock as less than human.

Comment [JB(]: AO2 – By describing lead as 'base', Arragon is using unnecessarily condescending language. He has immediately adopted an arrogant position of superiority, which will hamper him when it comes to making the right

'Who chooseth me must give and hazard all he hath.'
You shall look fairer, ere I give or hazard.
What says the golden chest? ha! let me see:
'Who chooseth me shall gain what many men desire.'
What many men desire! that 'many' may be meant
By the fool multitude, that choose by show,
Not learning more than the fond eye doth teach;
Which pries not to the interior, but, like the martlet,
Builds in the weather on the outward wall,
Even in the force and road of casualty.
I will not choose what many men desire,
Because I will not jump with common spirits
And rank me with the barbarous multitudes.
Why, then to thee, thou silver treasure-house;
Tell me once more what title thou dost bear:
'Who chooseth me shall get as much as he deserves:'
And well said too; for who shall go about
To cozen fortune and be honourable
Without the stamp of merit? Let none presume
To wear an undeserved dignity.
O, that estates, degrees and offices
Were not derived corruptly, and that clear honour
Were purchased by the merit of the wearer!
How many then should cover that stand bare!
How many be commanded that command!
How much low peasantry would then be glean'd
From the true seed of honour! and how much honour
Pick'd from the chaff and ruin of the times
To be new-varnish'd! Well, but to my choice:
'Who chooseth me shall get as much as he deserves.'
I will assume desert. Give me a key for this,
And instantly unlock my fortunes here.

Comment [JB(]: AO1 – Arragon shows his arrogance by suggesting that the lead casket should 'look fairer' if he is to risk failing in the casket test by choosing it.

Comment [JB(]: AO1 – Once again, Arragon's arrogance makes him brand 'many' as 'the fool multitude'. This is ironic, given the fate that awaits him.

Comment [JB(]: AO1 – Arragon condemns 'the fool multitude', whom he believes are easily influenced by appearances, judging by the exterior

Comment [JB(]: AO3 – In 'Macbeth' (1606), the 'temple-haunting martlet' is considered a good omen, as King Duncan approaches Macbeth's castle. However,

Comment [JB(]: AO2 – The simile 'like the martlet' only serves to show Arragon's arrogance, for he criticises the house martin's tendency to build their

Comment [JB(]: AO1 – Arragon is extremely arrogant when he calls other suitors 'common' and 'barbarous. The audience may hope he gets his just

Comment [JB(]: AO2 – The personification of 'fortune' emphasises that it is wrong to 'cozen' or cheat luck. Arragon's rhetorical question adds to the

Comment [JB(]: AO2 – Alliteration makes it appear that Arragon is so proud that, in his opinion, he does not 'wear an undeserved dignity'. Ironically, he does,

Comment [JB(]: AO2 – Repetition of the word 'merit' only serves as a reminder to the audience that Arragon is virtually devoid of merits, no matter how much he

Comment [JB(]: AO2 – Arragon uses the anaphora of the phrase 'How many' to make himself appear intelligent, but only succeeds in making himself look

Comment [JB(]: AO1 – The audience learns that pride comes before a fall, as Arragon decides to 'assume desert' or reward. In the end, he is made to look

2 CONTEXT & TEXT SUMMARY

CONTEXT

Although mentioning context is not as important as language analysis and responding to the question, it is, nevertheless, a good starting point. If you can understand some of the reasons why Shakespeare may have written the way he did, it should enhance your understanding of the text.

Although dates are not exact, the years when *The Merchant of Venice* was written was between 1596 and 1598. The reigning monarch at the time was the ageing, unmarried and childless Elizabeth I, who had been on the throne for forty years, during which time Protestantism was the official religion.

Unsurprisingly, religion is an important theme that you will encounter in the play. You must also remember that Shakespeare performed and wrote plays for the Queen, as a member of the Lord Chamberlain's Men. As the name suggests, all the actors were men during Shakespeare's time, so when female characters cross-dressed, they were, in fact, reverting back to their original gender! Of course, that aspect is lost in most modern productions of Shakespearean plays, which tend to have a unisex cast.

In fact, it is not unusual for Shakespeare's plays to have cross-dressing female characters. *The Two Gentlemen of Verona* (1594), *As You Like It* (1600) and *Twelfth Night* (1600) are three comedies that employ this plot device. However, there is much debate about whether or not *The Merchant of Venice* is a comedy. Due to the tragic elements in it, the play is often described as a tragicomedy.

However, from a contextual point of view, we could say that Shakespeare was deliberately empowering females, particularly at a time when the monarch was female. Like Elizabeth I, cross-dressing women in Shakespearean plays are portrayed as active, determined and intelligent.

Now let's consider the settings: Venice was considered to be a stylish place, whereas Belmont is fictional. This implies that there is tension between the male-dominated, public practicalities of money and the female-dominated, private fantasy world of romance. The differences between England and Venice was marked and perhaps the most relevant aspect to remark upon was that the Italian city-state was more international and had a large number of Jews living there. By contrast, three hundred years before Shakespeare's time, Jews had been officially banished from England. However, a couple of years before the play was performed, a Jewish doctor named Roderigo Lopez was executed for allegedly attempting to poison the Queen.

Even before this event, it was already common to blame Jews for all manner of afflictions, even the plague. They were an easy target to attack, as before their banishment, some had accumulated a lot of wealth from money-lending. Perhaps because of the official Christian position on charging interest, the word 'Jew' had become a term of verbal abuse for money-lenders, who were less than generous with their terms for repayment. In Elizabethan England, the legal amount of interest on a loan had to be ten percent or less, whereas in rich Venice, the amount to repay could be more than double or quadruple that interest rate. Therefore, to Elizabethans, all loans repayable with interest in Venice would have been considered usurious and sinful.

The original source of Shakespeare's play is thought to be a story called: 'Il Pecorone', which means 'blockhead'. It is about a young man called Gianetto, who attempts to woo the Widow of Belmont, using money borrowed from his friend, Ansaldo. As in Shakerspeare's play, Ansaldo has to use a Jewish money-lender to finance Gianetto. Other similarities include the 'pound of flesh' bond and a cross-dressing lawyer.

Act 1 Scene 1

The scene begins with Antonio bemoaning the fact that he doesn't know why he's so sad: 'I know not why I am so sad' (1). He admits that he doesn't understand himself: 'I must not understand myself very well' (7). We know he is melancholy, but we don't know why. It feels as if the play has begun in mid-conversation, or if it were a novel it would be described as in media res.

Salarino claims that Antonio's 'mind is tossing on the ocean', which alludes to his merchant ships at sea (8). Salarino seems to admire Antonio and his business enterprise, as, using a simile, he compares the ships to 'signors and rich burghers' (10).

Solanio, meanwhile, appears to mildly rebuke Antonio for not being content. If he were in Antonio's shoe, he would be 'plucking the grass' to find out the wind's direction (18). In other words, he would be too busy to be worried.

By contrast, Salarino seems more respectful and understanding. He can easily imagine how Antonio's worries about 'his merchandise' might cause him anxiety (40).

However, Antonio denies that his merchant ships are the cause of his sadness. He admits he is hedging his bets, as his merchandise is not all in 'one bottom trusted' (42). He also denies that he is 'in love', when Solanio suggests that (46-7).

Solanio mentioned 'two-headed Janus', a Roman god, who is linked with the villainous Iago from Othello, which was written around a decade later (50). Perhaps Solanio is suggesting that Antonio is being two-faced in not revealing what is bothering him. He compares the condition to those who refuse to laugh even if a joke is declared hilarious by 'Nestor', a Greek king who was renowned for his seriousness (56).

As soon as Bassanio arrives, Solanio tells Antonio that they will leave him 'with better company' (59). It seems as if he's being ironic, as Solarino adds that he would have stayed had 'worthier friends...not prevented' him (61).

Bassanio notes that Solanio and Salarino are growing 'exceedingly strange' as they leave (67). Salarino's parting words: 'We'll make our leisures to attend on yours' suggests there is no bad blood between them. Perhaps it is the presence of Lorenzo or Gratiano that has caused Solanio and Salarino to leave.

Gratiano immediately points out that Antonio looks 'not well' (73). He interrupts Antonio midline and through stichomythia the idea that Gratiano is verbally dominant is effectively conveyed. Gratiano insists on playing 'The Fool', and a Shakespearean audience would expect such a character to speak the truth albeit in a comedic way (79).

Gratiano insists that silence is not necessarily golden or wise, which allows Lorenzo to state that he 'must be one of these same dumb wise men' as the former never lets him speak (106).

Lorenzo and Gratiano exit, which allows Bassanio to talk to Antonio privately about the former's 'secret pilgrimage' to a love interest (119).

Bassanio reveals that 'her name is Portia' (164). He ranks her as highly 'Cato's daughter, Brutus' Portia' (165). This allusion to the wife of one of Julius Caesar's assassins does not seem to augur well. Neither does the reference to how 'her sunny locks/Hang on her temples like a golden fleece' (168-9). Jason may have won the fleece and a wife called Medea, but in the myth his wife kills his children, so the comparison appears to be unflattering.

Bassanio appears to be foolish and over-confident, as he asserts: 'I should question less be fortunate' (175). Antonio promises to enquiry 'where money is' to help finance Bassanio's quest to gain the hand of Portia (184).

Act 1 Scene 2

The scene changes from Venice to Belmont, the garden of Portia's house. Like Antonio, Portia is bemoaning her predicament. Unlike Antonio, instead of sad, she is 'aweary of this great world' (1). It seems like another version of ennui.

Nerissa seems to warning Portia not to be so self-indulgent, saying 'competency lives longer' than 'superfluity' (8-9, 8). We wonder if she's being a little sycophantic, as she panders to Portia a little by saying that to 'starve with nothing' is on a par with having 'too much' (5-6, 5).

Portia finds some wisdom in those comments and realises that her problem is psychological. She admits that 'poor men's cottages' can become 'princes' palaces' if people perceive them to be thus (12). The plosive 'p' in these alliterative lines seem borne of frustration. She is honest enough to realise it's difficult to practise what you preach or 'follow' your 'own teaching' (15). The nub of her problem is that her 'will' has been 'curbed by the will of a dead father' (21). The repetition of 'will' implies she has plenty of will-power, but is powerless in this situation.

Nerissa seems a little pessimistic about Portia's chances of finding true love as she says: 'The lottery that he hath devised...will no doubt never be chosen by any rightly' (24-27). This foreshadows the idea that Portia must help her favourite suitor to succeed.

Nerissa asks about the Neapolitan prince, to which Portia bawdily replies: 'I am much afeared my lady that his mother played false with a smith' (36-7). Portia is suggesting that he was born out of wedlock and loves horses because his real father was a blacksmith. The sexual and lewd content in her speeches here make prose more appropriate than verse.

Portia complains about her other suitors: the County Palatine does 'nothing but frown' (39); the copycat, Monsieur Le Bon 'is every man in no man' (49); the poor linguist, Falconbridge 'hath neither Latin, French, nor Italian' but has boxed 'the ear' of the Scottish lord (57, 65); while the drunkard Duke of Saxony's nephew is likened to 'a sponge' (81). Unsurprisingly, Portia thinks she 'will die as chaste as Diana', the Roman goddess of virginity, even if she lives to be as old as the Greek prophetess, Sibylla (87). These comments would have been well received by the reigning monarch at the time, Elizabeth I, who remained unmarried, but like Portia was inundated with suitors.

Portia unconvincingly pretends she cannot remember 'a Venetian, a scholar and a soldier' (92-3). However, initially, her enthusiasm gets the better of her, as she replies to Nerissa's enquiry: 'Yes, yes, it was Bassanio! - as I think so was he called'.

Her reaction to Bassanio is in stark contrast to her comment about the latest suitor: the Prince of Morocco. Portia would rather he 'shrive' than 'wive' her, with the rhyme emphasising how unpalatable it would be to marry someone with 'the complexion of the devil' (108, 107). These views reflect Elizabethan ideas about the beauty of skin colour, as it was not uncommon for women to apply lead to their skins to make themselves whiter and therefore more beautiful, in their eyes.

Act 1 Scene 3

The scene reverts to Venice and again we appear to be in mid-conversation as Shylock ponders Bassanio's request. Shylock continually repeats the word 'well' and the request for 'three thousand ducats for three months' (1, 3, 5, 8). It's almost as if Shylock cannot believe his good fortune to have Antonio 'bound' for this loan (9).

Perhaps because of the base nature of money-lending, their conversation is in prose. Shylock believes that Antonio may struggle to pay the sum back as 'his means are in supposition' (14-15).

Although he is keen to seal a deal, Shylock refuses to 'eat...drink' or 'pray' with Bassanio and Antonio for religious reasons (30). Shylock's mention of Jesus Christ conjuring 'the devil' by allowing Christians to eat pork would not have been well received by an Elizabethan audience (28).

Shylock's aside shortly afterwards allows him to confide with the audience, but Elizabethans may have offended by his reasons for hating Antonio 'for he is a Christian' (34). However, they may have been amused by his comments about Antonio looking 'like a fawning publican' or taxman, as that would play to the stereotype of Jews hating to part with money (33). Audiences may have seen Shylock as the stereotypical villain they would love to hate.

Despite being a stereotypical money-grabber, Shylock is not selfish. He thinks of his religion and the implications of forgiving Antonio when he says: 'Cursed be my tribe if I forgive him!' (42-43).

Since Antonio's entry, the language has switched from prose to verse, which suggests that the subject matter is more lofty than money-lending. However, Shylock links religion with profit when he says: 'thrift is blessing' while commenting on the Biblical story of Jacob from the Old Testament (82).

Antonio seems unimpressed by Shylock's Biblical references as he says: 'the devil can cite Scripture for his purpose' (90). Clearly, Antonio doesn't trust Shylock, but he is over-confident enough to underestimate him, perhaps.

The audience may begin to sympathise more with Shylock, as he mentions how Antonio has spat upon his 'Jewish gaberdine' and has voided his 'rheum upon' his 'bears' (104, 109). These graphic descriptions are not denied by Antonio, so it casts the latter into a less than flattering light.

Antonio shows no remorse and says that he is 'like to call' Shylock a dog 'again' (122). This shows how deep prejudice runs in Venetian society.

When the harsh terms of the bond are divulged, Bassanio honourably says to Antonio: 'You shall not seal to such a bond for me' (147). However, Antonio is guilty of over-confidence as he says: 'I will not forfeit it' (149).

Antonio continues in this overconfident vein, foreshadowing the future with a Gentile pun, calling Shylock 'the gentle Jew', who 'will turn Christian' (170, 171).

Act 2 Scene 1

The Prince of Morocco asks Portia to see past his 'complexion' and he uses the semantic field of war to convince her of his qualities. He calls his skin colour the 'shadowed livery' or uniform 'of the burnished sun' and brags that he can terrify the brave or 'valiant' (1, 2, 9).

Using stichomythia, Shakespeare implies Morocco's dominance over Portia and his unwillingness to listen to her. She may be ironic when she says he stands 'as fair/As any comer', but Morocco is too insensitive to pick up any nuances in her speech (20-21).

Morocco continues to brag in his war-like way of his exploits and his 'scimitar' which 'slew the Sophy and a Persian prince' (24-25). The sword may be a phallic symbol, showing that his love for her is more lust than deeply meaningful.

His vanity seems to know no bounds, as he sees himself as possessing Herculean strength, judging by his references to 'Hercules' and 'Alcides' (32, 35). However, even Morocco realises that 'blind Fortune' will dictate his future (36).

The scene ends with religious imagery, as Portia invites him 'to the temple' and he accepts that he will be 'blest - or cursed'st' (43, 46).

Act 2 Scene 2

Lancelot speaks in prose and reveals that he has two sides to his character: 'the fiend' and his 'conscience' (8, 10). This suggests that he may be untrustworthy.

Like Morocco, Lancelot acknowledges the power of Fortune, as he mentions 'fates and destinies' and 'the sisters three' in his speech to his father (50, 51).

He reveals his violent thoughts towards his former master, Shylock, when he says: 'Give him a halter!' (86). He reasons that he is 'famished' and is a 'Jew' himself, if he remains in Shylock's service (87, 91).

Like his father, Gobbo, Lancelot is prone to comic malapropisms, when he tells Bassanio that his 'suit is impertinent' rather than pertinent (113). In a sense, he is wooing Bassanio, who speaks in verse to show his superiority, as he wants to serve him rather than Shylock.

Lancelot acknowledges the power of 'Fortune' by personifying it as 'a good wench' (138, 139). This bawdy language is typical of the character.

Shortly after the clown's exit, Gratiano, the fool, enters. Bassanio describes the latter as 'too wild, too rude, and bold of voice' (152). It is almost as if the truth is frowned upon by those of a more romantic bent.

Gratiano uses the semantic field of religion to show him that he will be on his best behaviour should he go with him to Belmont. He mentions 'a sober habit', 'grace' and 'amen' to signal his intentions to be more respectful than usual (161, 164, 165).

Act 2 Scene 3

Jessica likens Lancelot to her father by calling him 'a merry devil' (2). This shows that he indeed becoming like Shylock by remaining employed by him. The audience can understand why she also wants to leave 'hell' (2).

Her guilt is obvious, though, as she recognises it is a 'heinous sin' to be 'ashamed to be' her 'father's child' (15, 16).

Act 2 Scene 4

Lorenzo asks Lancelot to tell 'gentle Jessica' that he will 'not fail her' (19, 20). Lorenzo uses alliteration and a pun on the word 'Gentile' to remind the audience that Jessica will have to change her religion to marry a Christian.

Whether or not it is genuine love is a moot point, as Lorenzo mentions the 'gold and jewels' that 'she is furnished with' (31). Nevertheless, he uses light imagery to describe her at the end of the scene, when he says: 'Fair Jessica shall be my torchbearer' (39). However, rather than romantic, it could be deemed as practical, as she will actually have to hold aloft the torch as they make off in the night.

Act 2 Scene 5

Shylock's descriptive triplet sounds decidedly unromantic, as he mentions that Jessica may 'sleep, and snore, and rend apparel out' (5). Before that, he suggests she has a tendency to 'gourmandise or over-eat' (3). This is either making Shylock sound mean, in that he resents his daughter eating so much which is costly, or it means she does actually eat too much.

Shylock warns her of succumbing to the 'shallow foppery' of the masque, which is ironic as she is about to do just that (34). Wearing a disguise, she is about to abscond or elope with Lorenzo.

Shylock's low opinion of Lancelot is evident, as he describes him as 'snail-slow', sleepier 'than the wildcat' and lazier than 'drones' who 'hive not' (45, 46). This implies that Shylock is an abusive employer.

Act 2 Scene 6

Gratiano uses bawdy language and nautical imagery to emphasise how more pleasure is gained from chasing love than gaining love. The 'strumpet wind' is blamed for causing wrecks, which intertwines the themes of love and money (17, 20).

When Jessica joins Lorenzo, she seems dismayed that she must indeed be the 'torchbearer' and 'hold a candle' to her 'shames' (41, 42). The light imagery seems to backfire on her, showing her in a boy's disguise and a less than romantic light.

However, Lorenzo calls her 'wise, fair and true', a triplet which suggests that he values her (57). Nevertheless, the mild oath he takes previously: 'Beshrew me' suggests that he thinks he may be the victim of a nagging wife if the marriage goes ahead as planned.

Act 2 Scene 7

Back in Belmont, Morocco is about to make his choice from 'several caskets', although there are only three (2). Perhaps, Portia is trying to exaggerate the task ahead to put Morocco off.

Morocco uses sea imagery to convey the idea that suitors have come from miles around to try their luck with Portia. He says: 'they come/As o'er a brook to see fair Portia' (46-47). He makes it sound like it is not really a huge ordeal to travel so far for such a beauty. Once again, the themes of fortune, riches and love are intertwined.

One of the most famously misquoted lines in Shakespeare appears inside the golden casket, as Morocco reads: 'All that glisters is not gold' (65). The alliteration emphasises how foolish he has been in making this choice.

Act 2 Scene 8

Back in Venice, Solanio describes Shylock as a 'dog', who is just as concerned with his lost 'ducats' as he is his 'daughter' (14, 15). Like Salarino, Solanio has no sympathy for Shylock and both ridicule his plight.

Solanio seems to lack sympathy for Antonio also, as he sees his sadness as self-indulgent, judging by his comment that they should relieve him of 'his embraced heaviness' (53).

Act 2 Scene 9

Returning to Belmont, we see the next suitor try his luck. Portia seems to give the Prince of Arragon a clue as she reminds him of the conditions of undertaking the task 'to hazard' for her 'worthless self' (17). The lead casket has the word 'hazard' on the inscription and lead is the least valuable of the three and therefore is the most 'worthless'.

Arragon uses a rhetorical question to emphasise his disappointment at choosing the wrong casket when he says: 'Did I deserve no more than a fool's head?' (58) At least he recognises that he already possessed 'one fool's head' when he 'came to woo', so the audience may have some sympathy for him (74).

Portia's comment that 'the candle singed the moth' reminds the audience that love is a dangerous game and a double-edged sword (78).

Meanwhile, Nerissa acknowledges that 'destiny' is the main reason why suitors fail rather than the 'wisdom' and 'wit' mentioned by Portia, which is not helping suitors to make the right choice (82, 80).

Act 3 Scene 1

Solanio begins by asking Salarino about the latest news from 'the Rialto', Venice's financial district (1). This makes Salarino seem more of a businessman or more knowledgeable of the two.

Salarino then has the opportunity to relay the news in prose that 'Antonio hath a ship of rich lading wrecked' (2-3).

Solanio's reaction is to describe Antonio as 'good' and 'honest', which makes the audience sympathise more with his losses at sea.

Shylock then enters, bemoaning his daughter's 'flight' (21). Salarino admits he knows 'the tailor' who 'made the wings' or her disguise, which allowed her to escape (22-23). Solanio comments that the 'bird was fledged', so Shylock should have expected nothing less. Bird imagery makes Jessica's actions appear natural, lessening any sympathy we may have for Shylock.

The Jew's anger is apparent in the repetition of the phrase 'Let him look to his bond' (37, 38, 39). It is almost as if he blames Antonio for what his daughter had done and now he want to take his vengeance out on him. It makes Shylock appear to be unreasonable.

Shylock reacts even more angrily to Salarino's rhetorical question about taking Antonio's 'flesh': 'What's the good for?' Shylock's response is full of rhetorical questions, including: 'Hath not a Jew eyes?' (46). This speech makes the audience question the racist way that Shylock has been treated and makes him appear to be the product of a deeply unfair and prejudiced society.

Tubal, another Jew, arrives to tell Shylock that he 'cannot find' Jessica (65). Although this makes the audience sympathise with Shylock, as he clearly has sent out friends to look for her in vain, his mercenary response makes him appear hard-hearted and callous. He wishes her dead with 'the jewels in her ear' and 'the ducats in her coffin' (70-71).

Nevertheless, it seems that Jessica has no sense of value, as she has traded 'a ring' for 'a monkey' (93, 94). Rings are very important in the play, as they symbolise loyalty amongst other things. Jessica regards the 'turquoise' ring she has been given by her father, which in turn was given to him by 'Leah', presumably his wife, as little more than a trinket (95-6, 96). She clearly does not appreciate what her father has done for her by bringing her up, which makes us think that either she's ungrateful or that Shylock is an abusive character, who has pushed her over the edge.

Act 3 Scene 2

We return to Belmont, where Portia is advising Bassanio to take his time. Although she says: 'a maiden has no tongue but thought', her advice is lengthy so contradicts her view that women should be seen and not heard (8). She even uses the phrase: 'Beshrew your eyes' that reminds the audience that she could easily become a shrew or nagging wife once she is married (14).

Bassanio tells her that waiting makes him feel in a torturous position, which he metaphorically likens to living 'upon the rack', a common form of Elizabethan torture for disloyalty to the Queen (25). The mythological reference to 'the virgin tribute paid by howling Troy' would have been well received by the reigning monarch, who was also unmarried and seemed surrounded by Herculean-type men hoping to win her favours (56).

While Bassanio prepares himself for the casket task, music plays with the lyrics warning against being taken in by 'fancy' personified or superficial appearances (63). This clues clearly leads Bassanio away from choosing gold or silver.

Bassanio absorbs the content of the message, decrying those that have 'the beards of Hercules' but 'livers as white as milk' (85, 86). We assume he is genuine and made of sterner stuff based on his comment.

It is easy for Bassanio to reject 'gaudy gold', as he remarks that it was 'hard food for Midas', the mythological king who regretted having the power to turn everything he touched to gold (101, 102).

Keeping in line with Elizabethan notions of beauty, which involved applying lead to the face to keep it white, he is moved by 'paleness' to choose the lead casket (106). Unsurprisingly, as the audience already know that gold and silver are the wrong choices, he finds 'fair Portia's counterfeit' or picture inside, which implies that the whole process of choosing has been unfair (115).

Portia's response to his success is modest, as she describes herself as 'an unlessoned girl', who 'may learn' and 'can learn' (159, 161, 162). Her humility is emphasised by her commitment 'to be directed' by Bassanio (164).

However, she invests a lot of importance in the ring she gives him, warning him that it will 'presage the ruin' of his love should he lose it (173). This brings home the enormity of what Jessica has done previously and will add tension later in the plot.

Gratiano's parallel courting of Nerissa makes the whole courtship process seem superficial, even more so as the couples appear ready to race against each other to have 'the first boy' (213). Bawdy innuendos about 'stake down' add to the feeling that Gratiano and Nerissa's relationship, at least, is far from serious.

However, Gratiano see himself as like Bassanio when he says: 'We are the Jasons, we have won the fleece' (240). That self-congratulatory tone is contrasted with the somber news that follows as Salerio reveals that Shylock is insisting on his pound of flesh from Antonio. The triplet emphasises the enormity of his 'envious plea of forfeiture, of justice, and his bond' (282).

Portia declares that she and Nerissa 'will live as maids and widows' until the matter is resolved (309). At this stage, it appears that the two females will conform to stereotype and remain at home while their new husbands work to save Antonio from death.

Act 3 Scene 3

Shylock begins by telling the silent jailer to 'look' at Antonio, 'the fool that lent out money gratis' without charging interest (1, 2). The audience must feel that Antonio's predicament is unenviable and that he has been let down by Fortune and Bassanio, who is not at hand to help.

Once again, we feel Shylock is a product of a harsh society that has treated him like a 'dog' as he now warns Antonio to 'beware' his 'fangs' (6, 7).

Using repetition, Shylock insists that he 'will have' his 'bond' (17). Solanio provides the biased commentary to this insistence, when he says: 'It is the most impenetrable cur/That ever kept with men' (17-18). The recurring dog imagery implies that if you treat people like animals they will behave like them, so perhaps the audience will understand Shylock's erroneous behaviour to some extent.

Act 3 Scene 4

Portia leaves Lorenzo to take control of 'the husbandry and manage' of her house in her absence as she claims that she intends 'to live in prayer and contemplation' accompanied by Nerissa (25, 28). She is conforming to the Elizabethan stereotype of women knowing their place although, of course, the reigning monarch did not conform to it herself.

Portia tells Nerissa bawdily that although they 'lack' the physical parts of men, they can more than compete 'these bragging jacks' (62, 77). This shows that despite her modesty, Portia is confident that in disguise she can match a man for ingenuity.

Act 4 Scene 1

The scene in the Duke's palace in Venice begins with the Duke describing Shylock as a 'stony adversary', which foreshadows the idea that Antonio is unlikely to receive mercy (4).

After Shylock enters the scene, the Duke mentions 'stubborn Turks' and 'Tartars', alluding to the Elizabethan perception that non-Christians are likely to show less mercy than Christians (32).

Shylock makes a strong case for not being merciful, by asking the rhetorical question: 'wouldst thou have a serpent sting thee twice?' He also reminds the audience that Christians have treated 'many a purchased slave' abjectly, purely because they feel they have ownership of another (90). He likens that to his demanding of 'the pound of flesh' from Antonio (99).

Bassanio's pleas to take his 'flesh, blood, bones, and all' instead of Antonio's falls on deaf ears, with the latter insisting that he is 'a tainted wether' or sick ram 'of the flock' (114). It seems that Bassanio, as a younger lamb of God, has more right to live his life.

Gratiano, meanwhile, mentions the Greek philosopher, 'Pythagoras', who claimed that souls could pass into another body after death (131). Gratiano suggests that Shylock's spirit is 'currish' or dog-like (133). It seems as if there can be no spiritual salvation for Shylock.

The Duke reads Bellario's letter aloud, which describes Balthazar as 'so young a body with so old a head' (160). This makes the audience and the court prepared for the disguised Portia's ingenuity.

Portia, disguised as Balthazar, makes a strong case for mercy, personalising it comparing it 'gentle rain from heaven' (181). It suggests that mercy is god-like and Shylock's lack of it implies that the Judaism is inferior to Christianity.

Shylock mistakenly considers Balthazar to be 'A Daniel come to judgement' (219). Ironically, Shylock believes that Balthazar will be like the legendary Jewish prophet, who was famous for revealing truth and promoting justice.

Fate appears to be siding with Shylock, as Antonio personifies Fortune as showing 'herself more kind/Than is her custom' (263-264). He is stoically accepting his fate, trying to convince himself that dying in this way is better than ageing without riches to comfort him.

Bassanio and Gratiano claim that Antonio's life is so valuable that their wives cannot be 'esteemed above' it (281). This creates comedy and dramatic irony for the audience know what the characters are unaware of: that their wives are witnessing their comments.

Portia's legal revelation that Shylock should 'shed no blood' in claiming his bond of a pound of flesh, prompts Gratiano to echo the Jew's words: 'I have you on the hip' (321, 330). This reminds the audience that the law is a minefield and words can be twisted to turn legal cases on their head.

Gratiano declares that Shylock should be afforded no mercy, when he says: 'A halter gratis' or a free hangman's noose should be the only mercy granted to the Jew. This seems hypocritical given how Christians are supposed to be more merciful that those of other religions.

Antonio insists that Shylock 'presently become a Christian' as part of the punishment (383). To add insult to injury, he also has to give all his possessions to 'his son Lorenzo and his daughter' once he dies (386).

Portia in disguise continues to be persuasive, saying to Bassanio that if his 'wife be not a mad woman', she would understand him giving his ring to the one who saved Antonio's life (441).

Bassanio is swayed by Portia's word and gets Gratiano to 'run and overtake' Balthazar, and give up the requested ring (448).

Act 4 Scene 2

Nerissa tries to compete with Portia, saying she'll see if she can get her 'husband's ring' (13). This makes the relationship appear a little childish.

Portia brags that they'll 'outface them', which shows that she is just as guilty as men in that respect (17).

Act 5 Scene 1

Lorenzo declares that 'the moon shines bright', but then mentions some mythological ill-fated romances (1). 'Troilus' was betrayed, 'Thisbe' never met her lover, 'Dido' was deserted by her lover, as was 'Medea' (4, 8, 10, 13).

Continuing with the same theme of difficult marriages, Stephano reveals that Portia is hoping for divine intervention to save her relationship with Bassanio. She 'kneels and prays/For happy wedlock hours' (31-32).

Lorenzo, meanwhile, talks of the power of music to uplift the spirit. It seems that Jessica is unaffected by it, as she reveals: 'I am never merry when I hear sweet music' (69). It implies she lacks a soul, so even her conversion to Christianity may not save their marriage.

Nevertheless, the pair are described as 'the moon' sleeping with 'Endymion' by Portia, when she sees them together (109). Superficially, at least, they appear to be well matched.

Portia explores the double meaning of 'light', as it meant unfaithfulness as well as having its more literal meaning during Shakespeare's time (129). Again, it seems to suggest that appearances can be deceptive.

After Gratiano insultingly reveals that he gave away his 'paltry ring' (147), he adds that his 'Lord Bassanio gave his ring away' too (179). This suggests that loyalty is not something that people can rely on.

Portia's reaction is bawdy, as she insists that she will 'know' the person who took the ring (229). By that, she means she will make love with Balthazar.

Gratiano plays on the stereotypical fears of Elizabethan men when he asks a rhetorical question: 'What, are we cuckolds ere we have deserved it?' (265). Men with unfaithful wives would have been taunted or worse during that era.

The happy ending you would expect of a comedy comes to fruition as Lorenzo describes Portia's news of the inheritance that he and his wife will gain as 'manna' from heaven (293).

The play finishes on a bawdy but comedic note, as Gratiano insists that his biggest concern is 'keeping safe Nerissa's ring' (307). This suggests that the couples have been driven together on a sexual level and may not have found themselves in lasting, meaningful relationships. This may have been well received by Elizabeth I, who was never married.

3 SAMPLE ESSAY QUESTION

Sample essay question

The AQA specimen paper I'm looking at asks students to read a 24-line extract:

Signior Antonio, many a time and oft

In the Rialto you have rated me

About my monies and my usances.

Still have I borne it with a patient shrug

For suff'rance is the badge of all our tribe.

You call me misbeliever, cut-throat dog,

And spit upon my Jewish gaberdine,

And all for use of that which is mine own.

Well then, it now appears you need my help.

Go to, then, you come to me, and you say,

'Shylock, we would have monies' – you say so,

You that did void your rheum upon my beard,

And foot me as you spurn a stranger cur

Over your threshold: monies is your suit.

What should I say to you? Should I not say

'Hath a dog money? Is it possible

A cur can lend three thousand ducats?'

Or Shall I bend low, and in a bondman's key,

With bated breath and whisp'ring humbleness,

Say this: 'Fair sir, you spit on me on Wednesday last,

You spurned me such a day, another time

You called me dog: and for these courtesies

I'll lend you thus much monies.'

Students are expected to read the extract and comment about how Shakespeare presents Shylock's feelings about how is treated in the extract and elsewhere in the play.

Okay, first things first, let's look at the question. The keywords are: 'feelings' and 'treated'.

At this stage, we need to concentrate on AO2, which deals with language, form and structure. If possible we need to use literary terms to describe the language that Shakespeare uses and, of course, we need to comment on the effects. If we can do that, we can score a maximum of 12 marks for AO2. The same applies to AO1, which concerns our personal response. Finally, if we can insert some comments about context we can score a maximum of six marks for those comments.

Annotated extract

Signior Antonio, many a time and oft

In the Rialto you have rated me

About my monies and my usances.

Still have I borne it with a patient shrug

For suff'rance is the badge of all our tribe.

You call me misbeliever, cut-throat dog,

Comment [M]: Venice's financial district.

Comment [M]: Means 'insulted' here and the alliterative 'r' with Rialto makes it sound like Shylock is growling like a dog, the animal he is constantly compared to.

Comment [M]: Shows his fixation on all things financial.

Comment [M]: Using money to make money. As Jews were banned from many other walks of life, many had few other options than to do this.

Comment [M]: Shows that he has put up with abuse patiently, shrugging it off as if it didn't hurt him.

Comment [M]: The personification of the word 'suff'rance' and its metaphorical transformation into a badge makes the pain he is feeling come to life.

Comment [M]: The prefix 'mis' suggests that his Jewish beliefs are wrong.

Comment [M]: Not only is he described as an animal, but more than that, Shylock has to deal with the compound adjective 'cut-throat', which is being applied to him. Ironically, later in the play, when he demands his 'pound of flesh', he lives up to the description. However, there is no reason to believe that he committed any acts that would be considered cut-throat prior to that. We can only assume that the epithet is gained from his practice of usury, which was frowned upon by Christians, particularly.

And spit upon my Jewish gaberdine,

And all for use of that which is mine own.

Well then, it now appears you need my help.

Go to, then, you come to me, and you say,

'Shylock, we would have monies' – you say so,

You that did void your rheum upon my beard,

And foot me as you spurn a stranger cur

Over your threshold: monies is your suit.

What should I say to you? Should I not say

'Hath a dog money? Is it possible

A cur can lend three thousand ducats?'

Or Shall I bend low, and in a bondman's key,

Comment [M]: This distinctive, long robe would mark Shylock out as a Jew and make him an easy target for abuse.

Comment [M]: The possessive pronoun 'mine' and the word 'own' make him seem to be a greedy character, who is unwilling to share.

Comment [M]: The word 'monies' is repeated from earlier in the speech, showing that money is an obsession for him.

Comment [M]: Although 'void' means 'expel' here, we enter the semantic field of the law here with the word's double meaning, as contracts can be torn up as

Comment [M]: This graphic description of Antonio spilling watery discharge from his nose onto Shylock's beard, shows the contemptible way the Jew has been

Comment [M]: 'Foot' is a verb here, meaning 'kick'. Normally, this word would be used metaphorically, as in 'kicking someone when they are down'. However,

Comment [M]: Shylock likens himself to a dog with this simile.

Comment [M]: The third repetition of 'monies' as a plural shows how important money is to Shylock.

Comment [M]: The use of a rhetorical question makes Shylock appear powerful, as he is making Antonio wait upon an answer.

Comment [M]: Another rhetorical question in quick succession makes Antonio and the audience think the probable answer to his 'suit' is 'no', as a

Comment [M]: The third rhetorical question mentions the sum, increasing the intensity of the effect by changing the dog imagery to the more offensive word;

Comment [M]: Although there is no question mark, a fourth rhetorical question shows how ludicrous it is for the abused Shylock to be approached for a

Comment [M]: This phrase meaning a 'slave's voice' shows how demeaning life is for Shylock in Venice.

With bated breath and whisp'ring humbleness,

Say this: 'Fair sir, you spit on me on Wednesday last,

You spurned me such a day, another time

You called me dog: and for these courtesies

I'll lend you thus much monies.'

> **Comment [M]:** The alliterative 'b' emphasises how much Shylock feels he is treated little better than a slave. The metaphor 'bated breath' shows he feels he usually has to moderate his breathing in Antonio's company.

> **Comment [M]:** The verb 'spurn' used to mean 'strike' as well as meaning to 'reject'. This adds to the impression that Shylock was physically as well as verbally abused by Antonio.

> **Comment [M]:** Shylock uses the word 'courtesies' ironically, as he has been far from treated politely by Antonio.

Activity: Looking at my annotations and using some of your own, now try to write an essay answering the question about how Shakespeare presents 'Shylock's feelings about the way he is treated'.

Here is my response, using the DAT (Definition, Apply, Terminology) introduction plan I gave you earlier.

The phrase: 'Shylock's feelings about the way he is treated' refers to his emotional response to others in Venetian society. In the play, Christians mostly abuse Shylock, but occasionally treat him as a potentially useful pariah and, unsurprisingly, the Jew is unhappy with the treatment. Shylock meets Antonio's request for money with rhetorical questions, which makes the latter think that his 'suit' is unlikely to be successful, while reminding the Christian that his behaviour has been far from exemplary.

Shylock feels he has been demeaned by Christian society. When he mentioned how Antonio has 'railed' him in the Rialto, the alliterative 'r' makes it sound like Shylock is growling like a dog, the animal he is constantly compared to. This is an example of him behaving like a dog because he feels forced to, due to his lack of status in Venetian society. This would subtly force even a contemporary audience to reconsider how they treat people of other religions and races.

Not only is he described as an animal, but more than that, Shylock has to deal with the compound adjective 'cut-throat', which has been applied to him. Ironically, later in the play, when he demands his 'pound of flesh', he lives up to the description. However, there is no reason to believe that he committed any acts that would be considered cut-throat prior to that. We can only assume that the epithet is gained from his practice of usury, which was frowned upon by Christians, particularly.

As well as having to contend with verbal abuse, it appears from Shylock's account that he has also been physically assaulted. Shylock has been the victim of a 'Foot' attack, which means 'kick'. Normally, this word would be used metaphorically, as in 'kicking someone when they are down'. However, here it appears to accurately portray what has happened in the past, as Antonio does not interrupt in protest. It could be argued that he is simply ready to listen as his purpose is borrow money and arguments about what happened in the past may jeopardize that. Nevertheless, the arguments made against Antonio are so graphic that it is hard to imagine how he can remain silently accused if there is not a lot of truth in Shylock's accusations. The Jew uses the word 'rheum' to emphasise how Antonio expelled mucous from his nose onto Shylock's beard. Although 'void' means 'expel' here, we enter the semantic field of the law here with the word's double meaning, as

41

contracts can be torn up as 'null and void'. In a sense, the pun 'void' foreshadows how Shylock is later tricked out of receiving his 'pound of flesh' as promised in 'the bond'. Clearly, Shylock is even unhappier at the end of the play at the perceived harsh injustice that he faces at the hands of the Christians, who insist on converting him to Christianity. Given the speculation that surrounds Shakespeare's religious views, at a time when being a Catholic could lead to dangerous accusations, it can be argued that the playwright sympathised with Shylock's situation. Despite the fact that Jews has been expelled from England, perhaps some of the contemporary audience would have also sympathised with the harsh treatment of the outsider, who feels completely alienated by society and Venice's judicial system.

Meanwhile, the depth of Shylock's feeling about the physical abuse he has suffered is revealed in the alliterative lines about 'bated breath', 'bend low' and a 'bondsman's key' The alliterative 'b' emphasises how much Shylock feels he is treated little better than a slave. The metaphor 'bated breath' shows he feels he usually has to moderate his breathing in Antonio's company, which highlights the inequalities in Venetian society. The plosive recurring 'b' sound implies that Shylock has had to repress his emotions for so long, but now he has the upper hand on Antonio he is allowing his feelings to be expressed with this succession of 'b' words.

Finally, the use of rhetorical questions, for example: 'What should I say to you?' makes Shylock appear powerful for once and able to turn the tables on his abusers, as he is making Antonio wait upon an answer. Another rhetorical question: 'Hath a dog money?' in quick succession makes Antonio and the audience think the probable answer to the latter's 'suit' is 'no', as a dog has no 'money'. It also forces Antonio to reflect on how poorly he has treated Shylock in the past and how the Jew cannot forget the harsh treatment that has left an indelible scar on his psyche. The third rhetorical question mentions the sum 'three thousand ducats', increasing the intensity of the effect by changing the dog imagery to the more offensive word: 'cur'. Although there is no question mark, a fourth rhetorical question: 'Or shall I bend low' shows how ludicrous it is for the abused Shylock to be approached for a favour. In Venice's unequal society, the abused Shylock feels as if he is still expected to be Antonio's humble servant and pretend as if nothing has happened previously, if he must 'bend low' and give in to the latter's request.

To conclude, Shylock uses an alliterative 'r' to show how he has learned to growl like a dog, presumably due to the abuse he has received at the hands of Christians. He bears a grudge, it seems, particularly as he has been the victim of a 'foot' and 'rheum' attack. The depth of Shylock's feeling about the physical abuse he has suffered is revealed in the alliterative 'b's. Rhetorical questions are arguably the most effective in revealing Shylock's emotional state, as he turns from downtrodden Jew to powerful money-lender. He seems to enjoy his moment of power, but ultimately he is destined for more 'suff'rance'.

Activity: look through the essay or your own and mark it for AO1, AO2 and AO3.

The phrase: 'Shylock's feelings about the way he is treated' refers to his emotional response to others in Venetian society. In the play, Christians mostly abuse Shylock, but occasionally treat him as a potentially useful pariah and, unsurprisingly, the Jew is unhappy with the treatment. Shylock meets Antonio's request for money with rhetorical questions, which makes the latter think that his 'suit' is unlikely to be successful, while reminding the Christian that his behaviour has been far from exemplary.

Shylock feels he has been demeaned by Christian society. When he mentioned how Antonio has 'railed' him in the Rialto, the alliterative 'r' makes it sound like Shylock is growling like a dog, the animal he is constantly compared to. This is an example of him behaving like a dog because he feels forced to, due to his lack of status

Comment [M]: AO3

Comment [M]: AO1

Comment [M]: AO2

Comment [M]: AO2

in Venetian society. This would subtly force even a contemporary audience to reconsider how they treat people of other religions and races.

Not only is he described as an animal, but more than that, Shylock has to deal with the compound adjective 'cut-throat', which has been applied to him. Ironically, later in the play, when he demands his 'pound of flesh', he lives up to the description. However, there is no reason to believe that he committed any acts that would be considered cut-throat prior to that. We can only assume that the epithet is gained from his practice of usury, which was frowned upon by Christians, particularly.

As well as having to contend with verbal abuse, it appears from Shylock's account that he has also been physically assaulted. Shylock has been the victim of a 'Foot' attack, which means 'kick'. Normally, this word would be used metaphorically, as in 'kicking someone when they are down'. However, here it appears to accurately portray what has happened in the past, as Antonio does not interrupt in protest. It could be argued that he is simply ready to listen as his purpose is borrow money and arguments about what happened in the past may jeopardize that. Nevertheless, the arguments made against Antonio are so graphic that it is hard to imagine how he can remain silently accused if there is not a lot of truth in Shylock's accusations. The Jew uses the word 'rheum' to describe how Antonio expelled mucous from his nose onto Shylock's beard. Although 'void' means 'expel' here, we enter the semantic field of the law here with the word's double meaning, as contracts can be torn up as 'null and void'. In a sense, the pun 'void' foreshadows how Shylock is later tricked out of receiving his 'pound of flesh' as promised in 'the bond'. Clearly, Shylock is even unhappier at the end of the play at the perceived harsh injustice that he faces at the hands of the Christians, who insist on converting him to Christianity. Given the speculation that surrounds Shakespeare's religious views, at a time when being a Catholic could lead to dangerous accusations, it can be argued that the playwright sympathised with Shylock's situation. Despite the fact that Jews has been expelled from England, perhaps some of the contemporary audience would have also sympathised with the harsh treatment of the outsider, who feels completely alienated by society and Venice's judicial system.

Meanwhile, the depth of Shylock's feeling about the physical abuse he has suffered is revealed in the alliterative lines about 'bated breath', 'bend low' and a 'bondsman's key' The alliterative 'b' emphasises how much Shylock feels he is treated little better than a slave. The metaphor 'bated breath' shows he feels he usually has to moderate his breathing in Antonio's company, which highlights the inequalities in Venetian society. The plosive recurring 'b' sound implies that Shylock has had to repress his emotions for so long, but now he has the upper hand on Antonio he is allowing his feelings to be expressed with this succession of 'b' words.

Finally, the use of rhetorical questions, for example: 'What should I say to you?' makes Shylock appear powerful for once and able to turn the tables on his abusers, as he is making Antonio wait upon an answer. Another rhetorical question: 'Hath a dog money?' in quick succession makes Antonio and the audience think the probable answer to the latter's 'suit' is 'no', as a dog has no 'money'. It also forces Antonio to reflect on how poorly he has treated Shylock in the past and how the Jew cannot forget the harsh treatment that has left an indelible scar on his psyche. The third rhetorical question mentions the sum 'three thousand ducats', increasing the intensity of the effect by changing the dog imagery to the more offensive word: 'cur'. Although there is no question mark, a fourth rhetorical question: 'Or shall I bend low' shows how ludicrous it is for the abused Shylock to be approached for a favour. In Venice's unequal society, the abused Shylock feels as if he is still expected to be Antonio's humble servant and pretend as if nothing has happened previously, if he must 'bend low' and give in to the latter's request.

Comment [M]: AO3
Comment [M]: AO3
Comment [M]: AO2
Comment [M]: AO2
Comment [M]: AO3
Comment [M]: AO2
Comment [M]: AO1
Comment [M]: AO2
Comment [M]: AO1
Comment [M]: AO1
Comment [M]: AO3
Comment [M]: AO3
Comment [M]: AO2
Comment [M]: AO2
Comment [M]: AO2
Comment [M]: AO2
Comment [M]: AO1
Comment [M]: AO1
Comment [M]: AO1

To conclude, Shylock uses an alliterative 'r' to show how he has learned to growl like a dog, presumably due to the abuse he has received at the hands of Christians. He bears a grudge, it seems, particularly as he has been the victim of a 'foot' and 'rheum' attack. The depth of Shylock's feeling about the physical abuse he has suffered is revealed in the alliterative 'b's. Rhetorical questions are arguably the most effective in revealing Shylock's emotional state, as he turns from downtrodden Jew to powerful money-lender. He seems to enjoy his moment of power, but ultimately he is destined for more 'suff'rance'.

AO1: Personal response

AO2: The writer's effect

AO3: Context

Comment [M]: AO1

Comment [M]: AO1

4 GLOSSARY

Glossary

Allegory: extended metaphor, like the grim reaper representing death, e.g. Scrooge symbolizing capitalism.

Alliteration: same consonant sound repeating, e.g. 'She sells sea shells'.

Allusion: reference to another text/person/place/event.

Ascending tricolon: sentence with three parts, each increasing in power, e.g. 'ringing, drumming, shouting'.

Aside: character speaking so some characters cannot hear what is being said. Sometimes, an aside is directly to the audience. It's a dramatic technique which reveals the character's inner thoughts and feelings.

Assonance: same vowel sounds repeating, e.g. 'Oh no, won't Joe go?'

Bathos: abrupt change from sublime to ridiculous for humorous effect.

Blank verse: lines of unrhymed iambic pentameter.

Compressed time: when the narrative is fast-forwarding through the action.

Descending tricolon: sentence with three parts, each decreasing in power, e.g. 'shouting, talking, whispering'.

Denouement: tying up loose ends, the resolution.

Diction: choice of words or vocabulary.

Didactic: used to describe literature designed to inform, instruct or pass on a moral message.

Dilated time: opposite compressed time, here the narrative is in slow motion.

Direct address: second person narrative, predominantly using the personal pronoun 'you'.

Dramatic action verb: manifests itself in physical action, e.g. I punched him in the face.

Dramatic irony: audience knows something that the character is unaware of.

Ellipsis: leaving out part of the story and allowing the reader to fill in the narrative gap.

End-stopped lines: poetic lines that end with punctuation.

Epistolary: letter or correspondence-driven narrative.

Flashback/Analepsis: going back in time to the past, interrupting the chronological sequence.

Flashforward/Prolepsis: going forward in time to the future, interrupting the chronological sequence.

Foreshadowing/Adumbrating: suggestion of plot developments that will occur later in the narrative.

Gothic: another strand of Romanticism, typically with a wild setting, a sensitive heroine, an older man with a 'piercing gaze', discontinuous structure, doppelgangers, guilt and the 'unspeakable' (according to Eve Kosofsky Sedgwick).

Hamartia: character flaw, leading to that character's downfall.

Hyperbole: exaggeration for effect.

Iambic pentameter: a line of ten syllables beginning with a lighter stress alternating with a heavier stress in its perfect form, which sounds like a heartbeat. The stress falls on the even syllables, numbers: 2, 4, 6, 8 and 10, e.g. 'When now I think you can behold such sights'.

Intertextuality: links to other literary texts.

Irony: amusing or cruel reversal of expected outcome or words meaning the opposite to their literal meaning.

Manichaean imagery: images of darkness juxtaposed with images of light, usually to show the battle of good versus evil.

Metafiction/Romantic irony: self-conscious exposure of the devices used to create 'the truth' within a work of fiction.

Motif: recurring image use of language or idea that connects the narrative together and creates a theme or mood, e.g. 'green light' in *The Great Gatsby*.

Oxymoron: contradictory terms combined, e.g. deafening silence.

Pastiche: imitation of another's work.

Pathetic fallacy: a form of personification whereby inanimate objects show human attributes, e.g. 'the sea smiled benignly'. The originator of the term, John Ruskin in 1856, used 'the cruel, crawling foam', from Kingsley's *The Sands of Dee*, as an example to clarify what he meant by the 'morbid' nature of pathetic fallacy.

Personification: concrete or abstract object made human, often simply achieved by using a capital letter or a personal pronoun, e.g. 'Nature', or describing a ship as 'she'.

Pun/Double entendre: a word with a double meaning, usually employed in witty wordplay but not always.

Retrospective: account of events after they have occurred.

Romanticism: genre celebrating the power of imagination, spriritualism and nature.

Semantic/lexical field: related words about a single concept, e.g. king, queen and prince are all concerned with royalty.

Soliloquy: character thinks aloud, but is not heard by other characters (unlike in a monologue) giving the audience access to inner thoughts and feelings.

Stichomythia: when characters speak alternate single lines of verse. The effect often shows characters vying for control, with the one interrupting appearing to have the upper hand.

Style: choice of language, form and structure, and effects produced.

Synecdoche: one part of something referring to the whole, e.g. Carker's teeth represent him in *Dombey and Son*.

Syntax: the way words and sentences are placed together.

Tetracolon climax: sentence with four parts, culminating with the last part, e.g. 'I have nothing to offer but blood, toil, tears, and sweat ' (Winston Churchill).

ABOUT THE AUTHOR

Joe Broadfoot is a secondary school teacher of English and a soccer journalist, who also writes fiction and literary criticism. His former experiences as a DJ took him to far-flung places such as Tokyo, Kobe, Beijing, Hong Kong, Jakarta, Cairo, Dubai, Cannes, Oslo, Bergen and Bodo. He is now PGCE and CELTA-qualified with QTS, a first-class honours degree in Literature and an MA in Victorian Studies (majoring in Charles Dickens). Drama is close to his heart as he acted in Shakespeare's 'Macbeth' and 'A Midsummer Night's Dream' at the Royal Northern College of Music in Manchester. More recently, he has been teaching 'Much Ado About Nothing' to 'A' Level students at a secondary school in Buckinghamshire, 'An Inspector Calls' at a school in west London, 'Heroes' at a school in Kent and 'The Merchant of Venice', 'The Sign of Four' and 'Blood Brothers' at a school in south London.

19358653R00035

Printed in Poland
by Amazon Fulfillment
Poland Sp. z o.o., Wrocław